GCE Applied Business:

Finance

Rewarding Learning

Colourpoint
Educational

☐ **Ian Bickerstaff**

ISBN: 978 1 904242 74 1

First Edition
First Impression

Layout and design: Colourpoint Books

Colourpoint Books
Colourpoint House
Jubilee Business Park
21 Jubilee Road
Newtownards
County Down
Northern Ireland
BT23 4YH

Tel: 028 9182 0505
Fax: 028 9182 1900
E-mail: info@colourpoint.co.uk
Web site: www.colourpoint.co.uk

Ian Bickerstaff is an experienced examiner, having acted as an assistant examiner for GCE Economics, and currently a principal examiner of both GCE Business Studies and GCE Applied Business. He is also a principal moderator of the Wider Key Skills. Ian has a combined Honours degree in Economics and Education and a Master's degree in Business Administration (MBA). He is employed as a university lecturer, teaching Accounting, Strategic Issues and Entrepreneurship. He is currently researching Entrepreneurship Education.

This book was edited by Eddie McKee. Eddie McKee is coordinator of Applied Business at St Louise's Comprehensive College, Belfast. He is also an experienced examiner for GCE Economics and GCE Applied Business. He is the author of another book in this series entitled *GCE Applied Business: External Influences*.

Acknowledgements

Thanks must go to a number of people without whose help this book would not have been completed.

Firstly to my wife Gail and my son Ryan for their unending patience and support; to my mother and father for their encouragement throughout the years; to Amanda Swann at CCEA and Julie Trouton at Colourpoint for their words of advice and encouragement.

CONTENTS

LIST OF ABBREVIATIONS

ARR – accounting rate of return

DPS – dividend per share

EPS – earnings per share

FRS – Financial Reporting Standard

NPV – net present value

ROCE – return on capital employed

SSAP – Statement of Standard Accounting Practice

VAT – value-added tax

CHAPTER 1

Sources of finance

All firms need finance in order to operate and grow and there is a range of ways that this finance can be raised. Each option will have its advantages and disadvantages and firms need to consider a number of factors when choosing the most appropriate source.

The finance can be categorised as either *internal* (for example, from the owner's savings and **capital**, or from **profits**) or *external* (for example, from a bank).

Sources of finance

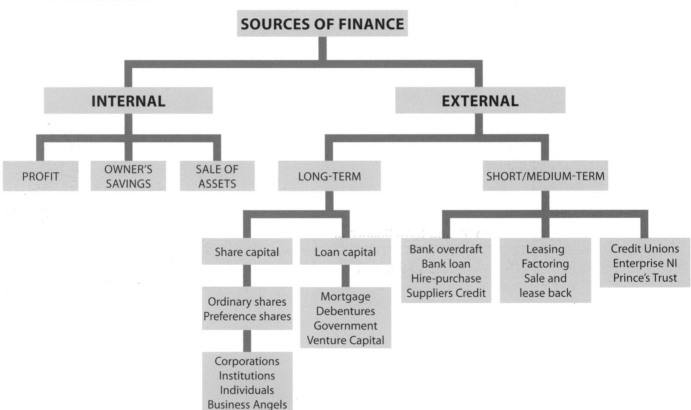

It is generally accepted that a business's borrowing requirements are matched to the expected life of the **assets** it is financing. The table below provides a guideline to these timescales.

Short-term	1–2 years	Short-term requirements such as working capital
Medium-term	3–10 years	Purchase of fixed assets such as a vehicle
Long-term	11–25 years	Purchase of land and premises

External sources of finance

We will now examine the range of sources of finance that are available to businesses.

☐ BANKS

Banks are the largest providers of finance to businesses and they can offer a wide range of different forms of finance.

Overdraft

An overdraft is a form of short-term borrowing. The bank will set a 'limit' up to which the business can borrow and this will generally be reviewed annually, although it is possible for the review period to be shorter. In return for granting an overdraft, the bank will charge the business an arrangement fee and interest.

An overdraft is the most common form of finance that a business can use to meet its short-term commitments such as paying other firms for goods or services that have been obtained on credit.

Business loan

A business loan is a fixed medium-term loan that is usually repayable after three to ten years. It is generally used to pay for capital items such as machinery and equipment. The firm will be expected to pay back the amount borrowed plus interest, in instalments.

©iStockphoto.com/tomazl Tomazi

Commercial mortgage

A commercial **mortgage** is a form of long-term finance and is typically used to buy premises and land. These assets are used as security for the loan, and if the business fails they will be sold to repay what is owed. A commercial loan is generally repaid in monthly instalments over a 25-year period.

Finance available from banks

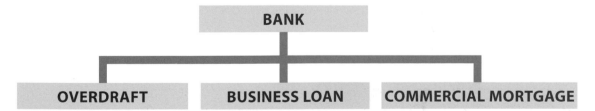

```
                    BANK
        ┌────────────┼────────────┐
    OVERDRAFT   BUSINESS LOAN   COMMERCIAL MORTGAGE
```

ACTIVITY 1.1

Choose a local bank and investigate the interest rate it charges for these three sources of finance. You should also highlight any special requirements that the bank may insist on.

HIRE-PURCHASE (HP)

HP allows a business to use an asset such as a computer or a photocopier without having to pay for it all initially. A finance house buys the asset from the supplier and retains ownership of it throughout the period of the HP agreement. The business pays a deposit for the asset and agrees to pay back the balance plus interest over the agreed period of time. At the end of the HP period the ownership of the asset passes over to the business.

LEASING

Leasing is also generally provided by a finance house. As is the case with HP, a business has use of the asset without having to buy it outright. However, the major difference between leasing and HP is that ownership of the asset does not normally pass over to the business.

A major advantage of this source of finance is that the business does not need to raise large sums of money and it can exchange the asset for a more modern version when technology changes. In addition, the maintenance and repair costs of the asset are not the responsibility of the business. However, over a long period of time leasing can be more expensive than the outright purchase of an asset.

FACTORING

When a company sells its goods or services on credit, it sends out an invoice which states the amount of money that is due. This invoice is evidence of the sale and the money owed to the company.

A factoring company will 'buy' these debts and will typically lend up to 80% of what is owed to the company that has sold the goods. The factoring company will deal with all of the paperwork associated with collecting the customer debts and will charge a fee, including interest and administration charges, in return. Factoring is therefore a useful source of short-term finance and can help to improve a firm's cash flow.

©iStockphoto.com/spxChrome

VENTURE CAPITAL

Venture capital companies offer advice and financial assistance to public limited companies looking for capital. The financial assistance can take the form of loans and venture capital which provide finance for **fixed assets** and **working capital**.

The venture capital company offers this assistance in return for **equity** and an element of control over the business, possibly through having a director on the board of the company. Although this is a quick and relatively cheap way of raising finance, its main drawback is that some control of the business will be lost.

The British Venture Capital Association (BVCA)

With 165 members, the BVCA represents the majority of UK-based private equity and venture capital firms. Since 1983, additional private equity invested in United Kingdom (UK) industry has amounted to £40 billion, with a further £14 billion invested in the rest of Europe. Those funds have gone to assist 25,000 UK companies. In 2002 alone, £5.4 billion was invested in 1,500 companies across Europe.

See the BVCA website for more information (www.bvca.co.uk).

(Adapted from www.bized.co.uk)

☐ SALE AND LEASEBACK

This involves an organisation selling its freehold property to an investment company and then leasing it back again over an agreed period of time. The major advantage of this is that funds are released for other uses.

☐ SUPPLIERS

If a firm can negotiate credit terms with its suppliers, this means money that would otherwise have been spent at the time of the sale can be used for alternative purposes.

☐ GOVERNMENT ASSISTANCE

Businesses can obtain loans and grants from the government for various purposes. Some of these may come from the European Union (EU), from UK national government, from regional government, or local government, or in some circumstances from National Lottery funds.

In Northern Ireland, Invest NI can provide assistance for local firms.

Parliament Buildings at Stormont

ACTIVITY 1.2

Investigate the Invest NI website (www.investni.com) and find out what types of financial assistance are available.

☐ ENTERPRISE NORTHERN IRELAND

Enterprise Northern Ireland provides both business start-up loans and business development loans.

ACTIVITY 1.3

Investigate the Enterprise Northern Ireland website (www.enterpriseni.com) and examine the criteria organisations must fulfil in order to obtain a loan.

☐ PRINCE'S TRUST

The Prince's Trust provides a range of assistance for 18–30 year-olds. This assistance includes market research grants, business start grants, business start-up loans, and business development loans.

ACTIVITY 1.4

Investigate the Prince's Trust website (www.princes-trust.org.uk) and examine the criteria organisations must fulfil in order to obtain a loan.

☐ CREDIT UNIONS

Some credit unions will provide loans to people who want to start a business. Such loans can only be granted to individuals on a personal basis, but they can then use the funds for the business.

☐ BUSINESS ANGELS

Business angels are informal investors who are looking to invest in new and growing businesses in return for a share of the equity. They usually have considerable experience of running businesses. They invest at all stages of business development, but most frequently invest in start-up and early-stage businesses. Most business angels tend to invest in businesses located within a reasonable distance of where they live.

☐ SHARE CAPITAL

Share capital is likely to be the most important source of funds for **limited companies** as the sale of shares can raise very large amounts of money.

©iStockphoto.com/shulz

Shareholders receive benefits from profits, in the form of cash **dividends** and through the possible increase in the value of their shares. Shareholders are owners of the business and they enjoy limited liability. This means that the maximum amount they can lose is the amount that they paid for the shares they hold.

It is possible for a limited company to issue different types of shares.

Ordinary shares

Ordinary shares are also known as equity shares and they are the most common form of share in the UK. An ordinary share gives the right to its owner to share in the profits of the limited company (dividends) and to vote at general meetings of the company.

Since the profits of companies can vary substantially from year to year, so can the dividends paid to ordinary shareholders. In bad years, dividends may be nothing whereas in good years they may be substantial.

Tesco plc share prices 13 February 2007

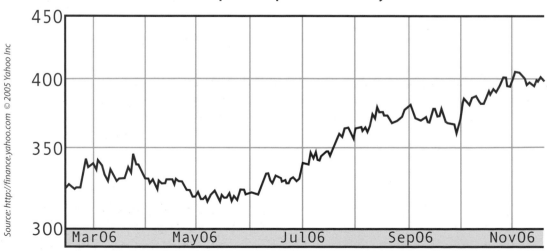

Source: http://finance.yahoo.com © 2005 Yahoo Inc

Preference shares

Preference shares entitle their owners to certain preferences over ordinary shareholders. There are two major differences between ordinary and preference shares:

- Preference shareholders are often entitled to a fixed dividend even when ordinary shareholders are not.
- Preference shareholders cannot normally vote at general meetings.

The preference dividend is fixed in the sense that preference shares are often issued with the rate of dividend fixed at the time of issue. If by any chance a company cannot pay its preference share dividend then it cannot pay any ordinary share dividend. This is because the preference shareholders always have the right to receive their dividend before the ordinary shareholders – hence the term 'preference'.

Preference shares are usually cumulative. This means that if one year's dividend is not paid, then it will be carried forward to the next year.

☐ DEBENTURES

Debentures are loans for limited companies that are usually secured. A secured debenture is one that is specifically tied to the financing of a particular asset such as a building or a machine. Then, just like a mortgage for a private house, the debenture holder has a legal interest in that asset and the company cannot dispose of it unless the debenture holder agrees. If the debenture is for land and/or buildings it can be called a mortgage debenture.

Debenture holders have the right to receive their interest payments before any dividend is payable to shareholders and, most importantly, even if a company makes a loss it still has to pay its interest charges, including interest on its debentures.

If the business fails, the debenture holders will be preferential **creditors** and will be entitled to the repayment of some or all of their money before the shareholders receive anything.

Liverpool agrees takeover offer

Liverpool has agreed terms of an offer for the club from the American consortium led by George Gillett and Tom Hicks. The Liverpool board have unanimously recommended that the club's shareholders accept the offer.

Liverpool chairman David Moores said "I believe this is a great step forward for Liverpool, its shareholders and its fans. This club is my passion and forms a huge part of my life. After much careful consideration, I have agreed to sell my shares to assist in securing the investment needed for the new stadium and for the playing squad. I urge all my fellow shareholders to do the same and to support the offer. By doing so, I believe you will be backing the successful future of Liverpool Football Club. I am also delighted to accept the offer from the Hicks and Gillett families to continue my involvement in the club by becoming Honorary Life President."

Arrangements over the future of Liverpool's new stadium appear to have clinched the deal. Not only has Hicks built up a reputation for developing state-of-the-art stadia for his teams, but the duo have now guaranteed that Liverpool's proposed new Stanley Park ground will not be shared with other teams. In Gillett's original approach, when he was considering a solo takeover, he had indicated he wanted a ground-share arrangement to cut costs and maximise income.

Hicks and Gillett will now split the £470 million cost of taking over the club on a 50-50 basis, with around £255 million going to buy the shareholding and take over the £80 million debt, and a further £215 million to be spent on the stadium. The takeover means Liverpool, Manchester United and Aston Villa will all be in American hands.

Commenting on the offer, Gillett and Hicks said "Liverpool is a fantastic club with a remarkable history and a passionate fanbase. We fully acknowledge and appreciate the unique heritage and rich history of Liverpool and intend to respect this heritage in the future. The Hicks family and the Gillett family are extremely excited about continuing the Club's legacy and tradition."

ITV have become the first of the other major shareholders to announce that they have also agreed to sell their stake – of 9.99% – in the club. A statement read "ITV plc today announces that it has given an irrevocable undertaking to sell its 9.99% shareholding in Liverpool Football Club and Athletic Grounds Plc at a price of £5,000 per share. This would result in cash proceeds of £17.4 million in the event that the offer for the club, announced today, becomes unconditional."

A statement released by Liverpool said "The boards of Kop and Liverpool are pleased to announce that they have agreed the terms of a recommended cash offer to be made by Kop to acquire the entire issued share capital of Liverpool. The offer is £5,000 in cash for each Liverpool Share, valuing the issued share capital of Liverpool at approximately £174.1 million. Together with the £44.8 million of net debt in the club as at 31 December 2006, this represents an enterprise value for Liverpool of £218.9 million."

(Adapted from the *Telegraph* website, 6 February 2007)

Internal sources of finance

Although the main sources of finance for an organisation are external, there are some internal sources that can be drawn upon.

☐ OWNERS' SAVINGS

A common source of finance, specially for **sole traders** and **partnerships**, comes from the owners' savings.

©iStockphoto.com/hidesy

☐ PROFIT/RETAINED EARNINGS

A firm's profit after tax is an important and inexpensive source of finance.

☐ SALE OF ASSETS

Sometimes a business will sell off assets to raise money. This may happen if the organisation has exhausted all other avenues of raising finance.

Choosing the source of finance

In choosing a source of finance there are a number of factors that a business needs to take into consideration:

- **Cost** – the business will need to examine how much the source of finance will cost it. This will require an analysis of both interest payments and administration costs.
- **Time** – the business will need to consider the length of time the finance is required for.
- **Flexibility of the finance** – this will involve examining how easy it is to transfer from one source of finance to another.
- **Status and size** – sole traders will be limited in their choice of finance whereas public and private limited companies will have a much wider choice.
- **Financial situation** – when a business is in a poor financial situation, it may find that providers of finance are more reluctant to offer finance, or even if they are willing, the cost may rise.

©iStockphoto.com/Yuri_Arcurs

REVISION QUESTIONS

1. Susan Anderson has set up a new business designing and selling mugs. She invested her savings of £10,000, but estimated that she needed an additional £10,000 in order to purchase fixed assets. Suggest one source of finance which would be suitable for Susan, giving a reason for your suggestion.

2. Explain the main external sources of finance available to a business, outlining the advantages and disadvantages of each.

3. Investigate the differences between a preference share and an ordinary share.

PAST PAPER QUESTIONS

1. Sources of business finance and Invest NI
    (a) (i) Explain three possible sources of finance available to a sole trader.   [6]
        (ii) Explain three possible sources of finance available to public limited companies   [6]

    (b) Study the information below and answer the question that follows.

    "Investment in supporting economic development projects by Invest NI leads to significant leverage of private sector funds and will help create more wealth, more jobs and enhanced economic activity – this is a key priority for creating a sustainable private sector economy in future ..."
    (Adapted from the *Business Telegraph*, Monday 18 April, 2005, Author: Robin Morton)

    Evaluate the role of Invest NI in assisting business within Northern Ireland.   [15]

PAST PAPER ANSWERS

1. (a) (i) Sole traders
    Owners' capital:
    • Personal savings; (money saved by owners of business); money from family members
    • Grants – from grant-awarding bodies, eg lottery, Invest NI, etc used to start the business
    Institutional funding:
    • Loans, from banks or relevant funding bodies; HP; overdrafts; mortgage
    • Retained profits
    • Working capital – trade credit
    • Sale of assets
    • Other appropriate sources   [6]
        ([2] for each item stated; [1] for identification; [1] for suitable explanation; 3x[2])
    (ii) Public limited companies.
    • Shares – capital issued by company to shareholders, subdivided into small amounts referred to as shares (preference or ordinary); return on shares referred to as a dividend; some shares (ordinary) carry voting rights
    • Debentures – loans to a company which must be repaid; carry an interest rate charge which also has to be paid; venture capital
    • Retained earnings – profits which the company has earned, which are brought forward from previous accounting periods; can be used to supplement sources of funding
    • Invest NI funding/assistance
    • Sale of assets   [6]
        ([2] for each item stated; [1] for identification; [1] for suitable explanation; 3x[2])
    (b) • Invest NI's mission is "to accelerate economic development in Northern Ireland, applying expertise and resources to encourage innovation and achieve business success, increasing opportunity for all within a renewed culture of enterprise"; ie to develop regional economy; job creation; reduce unemployed levels; grants.
    • Invest NI seeks to encourage innovation and entrepreneurship and create an environment in which all companies (home-grown and international) can flourish. This in turn will lead

to new levels of wealth that will benefit all who live in Northern Ireland.

- The agency focuses on measures that will help companies become and remain competitive in global markets – examples: trade missions; marketing advice; language training; contact information.

- It also seeks to provide innovative initiatives that help companies to improve on their capabilities. It realises that in a time of globalisation, where geographical distances are irrelevant, particularly for knowledge-based businesses such as computer software design, if Northern Ireland's potential is to be realised, then help is needed.

- Invest NI brought together organisations including former LEDU, IDB etc, and with this new structure it is believed that organisational synergies can be realised.

- The initiative to form Invest NI was taken by the then Minister for Enterprise, Trade and Investment, Sir Reg Empey, and consultation played a major part in the strategy development process.

- Alternatively, within the context of the case study material, candidates may suggest that Invest NI assistance is not required or not necessary.

- Candidates may present final judgement on the case study indicating that Invest NI assistance is more likely to be beneficial.   [15]

Level 1: ([1]–[6])

Some knowledge and understanding of the role of Invest NI (INI) is demonstrated but this knowledge is limited. Application of this knowledge to the question context, if present, is very limited. Limited evaluation of role of INI. Quality of written communication is limited. (Up to two points accepted.)

Level 2: ([7]–[12])

Adequate knowledge and understanding of the role of INI is demonstrated. There is some application of this knowledge to the question context. Some evaluation of role of INI. Quality of written communication is satisfactory. (Up to four points accepted.)

Level 3: ([13]–[15])

Thorough knowledge and understanding of the role of INI is demonstrated. There is good application of this knowledge to the question context. Thorough evaluation of the role of INI – a final judgement is required. Quality of written communication is of a high standard. (Five or more points accepted.)

CHAPTER 2

Financial statements for sole traders

A **sole trader** is an individual trading in his or her name, or under a suitable trading name. This is the most common form of business. Out of approximately 3.6 million businesses in the UK, over 2 million are sole traders.

Each year a business will draw up its final accounts. These accounts show the profits that a business has made and will list the business's **assets** and **liabilities**. These accounts are drawn up from a **trial balance.**

©iStockphoto.com/shulz

The trial balance

The trial balance is drawn up by the business's book-keeper who adds up all of the balances of its **debtors** and **creditors accounts**. These accounts will include sales accounts, purchases accounts, expenses accounts, creditors accounts, and debtors accounts.

The trial balance is a list of account balances, arranged in two columns according to whether they are debit balances or credit balances. When all of the balances are entered they are totalled and the total for both columns should be the same, as illustrated in the example below.

Trial balance as at 31 December 2007

	Dr £	Cr £
Bank	9,350	
Capital		15,000
Purchases	870	
Sales		475
Motor van	4,950	
Debtors	220	
Drawings	185	
Creditors		275
Insurance	175	
	15,750	**15,750**

Once the trial balance is drawn up it will be handed to the accountant who will prepare the **final accounts** of the business. These are known as final accounts because they are produced at the end of the financial year. The final accounts are made up of the **trading/profit and loss account,** and the **balance sheet**.

The trading account

The trading/profit and loss account may be subdivided into the **trading account** and the **profit and loss account**.

The trading account sets out the **gross profit** that the business has made and the profit and loss account sets out the **net profit** that has been made.

Gross profit is what the business has gained from trading (buying and selling). It is calculated by taking the difference between the firm's sales and the **cost of goods sold**.

gross profit = sales – cost of goods sold

The cost of goods sold is calculated by adding the opening stock (the stock that the firm has at the beginning of the trading period) to the purchases and subtracting the closing stock (the stock left over at the end of the trading period).

cost of goods sold = opening stock + purchases – closing stock

For example, Ciaran has been given a box of 48 Mars Bars by his uncle. Unfortunately, Ciaran does not like Mars Bars so he decides to sell them at a local car-boot sale.

At the sale he is offered another box of 48 bars at a knockdown price. He now has 96 bars. During the sale he sells 20 bars, leaving him with 76 bars.

Opening stock	48	
Add purchases	48	96
Less closing stock		76
Goods sold		20

If Ciaran values the Mars Bars at 30p each, his accounts would be as follows.

	£	£	£	
Opening stock	14.40			(48 × 30p)
Add purchases	14.40	28.80		(48 × 30p)
Less closing stock		22.80		(76 × 30p)
Cost of goods sold			6.00	(20 × 30p)

The table below for the fictional business 'Happy Burgers' is an example of a trading account.

Trading account of Happy Burgers for year ending 31 December 2007

	£	£	£
Sales			500,000
Opening stock	6,000		
Purchases	256,000	262,000	
Closing stock		10,000	
Cost of goods sold			252,000
Gross profit			**248,000**

It is important to note that sales and purchases only include items that are bought and sold during normal trading. They do not include items such as machinery or vehicles – these are classified as **fixed assets.**

The profit and loss account

This account subtracts from the gross profit figure any expenses that have been incurred. This gives the **net profit**.

net profit = gross profit – expenses

The profit and loss account looks at how well a firm has traded over the time period concerned (usually the last six months or year). It basically shows how much a firm has earned from selling its product or service, and how much it has paid out in costs (production costs, salaries, and so on). The difference between these two is the amount of profit that has actually been earned.

Profit and loss account of Happy Burgers for year ending 31 December 2007

	£	£	£
Gross profit			248,000
Less expenses:			
Wages and salaries		55,000	
Electricity		34,000	
Rent and rates		10,000	99,000
Net profit			**149,000**

It is normal practice to combine the trading account and the profit and loss account into a single format.

Trading and profit and loss account of Happy Burgers for year ending 31 December 2007

	£	£	£
Sales			500,000
Opening stock	6,000		
Purchases	256,000	262,000	
Closing stock		10,000	
Cost of goods sold			252,000
Gross profit			**248,000**
Less expenses:			
Wages and salaries		55,000	
Electricity		34,000	
Rent and rates		10,000	99,000
Net profit			**149,000**

The balance sheet

Before examining the layout of the balance sheet it is important to explore some of the accounting terms of items associated with it.

ASSETS

Assets are items which are owned by the business or money which is owed to the business. They fall into two groups.

Fixed assets

These are items which have a life span of more than one year. They are usually items that the business expects to keep. Fixed assets include land and buildings, plant and machinery, fixtures and fittings, and motor vehicles. These assets are fixed because they are necessary for the business to trade but are not affected by the level of trade or the profit made. If a business purchases any fixed assets then this is known as **capital expenditure.**

Current assets

Current assets are items that the business will hold for a much shorter term. The value of these items changes in proportion to the amount of trade that a business engages in. Current assets include **stocks** (raw materials, work in progress, and finished goods for resale), debtors (money owed to the business), bank balances, and cash in hand.

Current assets are often described as being more 'liquid' or having higher 'liquidity' than fixed assets. What this simply means is that assets of this type are much easier to turn into cash.

What are stocks?

Stocks are often also known as **inventories**. They are anything a firm has which is not currently being used for one of the firm's functions. Most departments in the company will have stocks of something. For example, in a single company the factory may have stocks of raw materials ready to produce, the office may have stocks of stationery, and the warehouse may have stocks of finished goods.

Stocks are vital to a company to help it function smoothly. If production had to be stopped every time a firm ran out of raw materials, the time wasted would cost it a lot of money. If a shop had no stock on the shelves, customers would soon start to go elsewhere. The same is true of most areas a firm operates in.

Stocks are considered to be current assets because many types of stocks can be converted into cash reasonably readily – particularly stocks of finished goods. However, they are generally the least liquid of the current assets. In a recession it may be very difficult for a firm to sell stocks, and so, although they may be listed as being of a certain value, their true value may be lower.

Trial balance of Watercress as at 31 December 2007

	£	£
Premises	240,000	
Long-term loan		120,000
Capital		140,000
Debtors	3,800	
Creditors		3,000
Drawings	10,000	
Cash	300	
Stock: 1 Jan 20-1	8,400	
Fixtures and Fittings	8,000	
Vehicles	16,000	
Bank overdraft		1,500
Sales		390,000
Purchases	308,000	
Wages	41,000	
Sundry expenses	1,900	
	654,500	**654,500**

Stock at 31 December 2007 was valued at £10,400.

Trial balance of Richard Allen as at 31 December 2007

	£	£
Debtors	18,600	
Creditors		17,960
Bank	5,000	
Capital		25,250
Sales		144,810
Stock: 1 Jan 20-1	16,010	
Salaries	18,465	
Heat and light	1,820	
Rent and rates	5,647	
Motor vehicles	9,820	
Office equipment	5,500	
Sundry expenses	845	
Motor expenses	1,684	
Drawings	13,311	
	188,020	**188,020**

Stock at 31 December 2007 was valued at £17,000.

☐ LIABILITIES

Liabilities are amounts that are owed by a business. They fall into two groups.

Long-term liabilities

These are loans that are repayable in more than one year. If the business premises were mortgaged, then that mortgage would be a long-term liability. In addition, the capital put into the business by the owner would be looked on as money owed by the business to the owner – another long-term liability.

Current liabilities

These are amounts owed by a business that must be repaid within 12 months. Current liabilities include money owed to creditors (for goods purchased but not yet paid for), money owed for services such as the telephone bill (often called **accruals** – see page 21), and bank overdrafts. You may think that an overdraft is repayable over a longer term but the bank can demand repayment at any time.

©iStockphoto.com/Duncan Walker

The **balance sheet** is one of the financial statements that organisations produce every year. It is like a snapshot of the organisation's financial situation at that moment in time as it is worked out at the organisation's year end, setting out the value of the business's assets and liabilities on the final day of the firm's financial year.

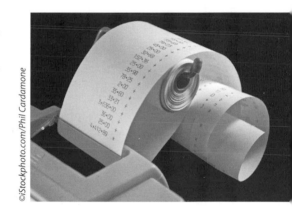

©iStockphoto.com/Phil Cardamone

It is given in two halves:
- The top half shows where the money is currently being used in the business (the net assets).
- The bottom half shows where that money came from (the capital employed).

The value of the two halves must be the same, ie capital employed = net assets.

The money invested in the business may have been used to buy fixed assets or current assets. The top half of the balance sheet will therefore be made up of the total of the fixed and current assets, less any current or long-term liabilities the firm may have.

You can see an example of a balance sheet overleaf.

Balance sheet of Happy Burgers as at 31 December 2007

	£	£	£
Fixed assets:			
Premises			45,000
Machinery			30,000
Motor vans			19,000
			94,000
Current assets:			
Stock	23,000		
Debtors	18,000		
Bank	10,000		
Cash	2,000	53,000	
Less current liabilities:			
Creditors		37,000	
Working capital			16,000
			110,000
Less long-term liabilities			50,000
Net assets			60,000
Financed by:			
Capital	50,000		
Add net profit	14,000	64,000	
Less drawings		4,000	60,000

Fixed assets are added together and the total is recorded in the third column of the balance sheet.

Current assets are added up and the total is entered in the middle column. Current liabilities are also added up and the total placed in the middle column. Current liabilities are subtracted from current assets and the resulting figure is recorded as working capital in the third column. If there are any long-term liabilities they are subtracted from fixed assets plus working capital to give net assets.

The bottom part of the balance sheet is recorded by adding together capital and net profit, and subtracting any **drawings**.

> Working capital = current assets – current liabilities
>
> Total fixed assets + working capital – long-term liabilities = net assets

Adjustments

The final accounts produced to date provide a basic statement of the profitability of an organisation and its balance sheet position. There are, however, a number of corrections that need to be made to these accounts to give a truer picture of the business. These corrections are known as adjustments.

©iStockphoto.com/Angel Herrero de Frutos

PREPAYMENTS

A **prepayment** is the part of an expense which is paid in advance for the next month or the next year.

An invoice included in the final reports may cover a period of the next financial year. For example, a firm may have an advertising expense of £1,200 for a year's public relations (PR) services. If the firm's financial year runs from January to December, but the PR company has billed the firm from June to June, £600 belongs to the next year.

> **Rule**
>
> Subtract the prepayment amount from the expenses in the trading/profit and loss account.
>
> Include the prepayment amount with the current assets in the balance sheet (it is an 'advantage' to the business as they have prepaid an expense).

For example, if electricity was £34,000, but £200 was prepaid, we reduce the electricity from £34,000 to £33,800 in order to ensure that the net profit is accurate. This is illustrated below.

	£
Trading/profit and loss account	
Subtract £200 from original expenses	
34,000 – 200	33,800
Balance sheet	
Current assets:	
Prepayment	200

ACCRUALS

An **accrual** (amount owing) is an expense that belongs to the current accounting period. Electricity often has to be accrued. For example, if the financial year is January to December, and the electricity bill for November and December arrives in January, some of the expense will belong to the last financial year. Firms usually estimate how much should be charged and make an accrual.

> **Rule**
>
> Add the amount of the accrual to the expenses in the trading/profit and loss account.
>
> Include the amount of the accrual with the current liabilities in the balance sheet (a firm must pay it so the firm is liable for it).

For example, if wages and salaries were £55,000, but the manager decided to accrue £500 because of an outstanding staff part-time claim, then wages and salaries must be increased to £55,500 in order to ensure that the net profit is accurate.

	£
Trading/profit and loss account	
Add £500 to existing wages and salaries expenses	
55,000 + 500 accrual	55,500
Balance sheet	
Current liabilities:	
Accruals	500

An accrual means that an expense is 'incomplete'. The manager will know from experience if an accrual needs to be made. For example, a department manager may receive an invoice for flowers and forget to send it to the accounting department, so in order to have an accurate net profit an accrual will need to be made.

ACTIVITY 2.1

State whether each of the following is an accrual or a prepayment.

1. The housekeeping supervisor of a hotel forgot to send an invoice for guest soap bars to the accounting department.
2. The marketing manager tells you that half of the advertising invoice belongs to the next accounting year.
3. An electricity bill for the last three months is expected to arrive any day.

After these adjustments the new layout of the trading/profit and loss account is shown below.

Trading and profit and loss account of Happy Burgers for year ending 31 December 2007

	£	£	£
Sales			500,000
Opening stock	6,000		
Purchases	256,000	262,000	
Closing stock		10,000	
Cost of goods sold			252,000
Gross profit			**248,000**
Less expenses:			
Wages and salaries	55,000		
Add accrual	500	55,500	
Electricity	34,000		
Less prepayment	200	33,800	
Rent and rates		10,000	99,300
Net profit			**148,700**

Note: The first column of the profit and loss account can be used to show the calculation, ie to add the accrual (amount owing) or to subtract the prepayment (amount still outstanding).

Accruals are included in the balance sheet as current liabilities and prepayments are included as current assets.

Both accruals and prepayments are found in the notes section of the trial balance.

SALES RETURNS AND PURCHASE RETURNS

Sales returns (also known as **returns inwards**) are goods that have been sold by the firm and then have been returned by customers. As the sales figure is no longer accurate these are subtracted from sales in the trading account.

Purchase returns (or **returns outwards**) occur when the business itself returns goods to one of its suppliers. As the purchases figure is no longer accurate this figure is deducted from purchases in the trading account.

DISCOUNT ALLOWED AND DISCOUNT RECEIVED

Discount allowed is the amount of discount given by a business to encourage debtors to pay promptly. It is treated as an expense and is entered in the trading/profit and loss account with other expenses.

Discount received is the amount of discount taken by a business when it settles its creditors promptly. This has the effect of increasing the amount of gross profit that the firm makes and it is therefore added to the gross profit figure in the trading/profit and loss account.

RENT RECEIVED

This is income that is received from renting out assets belonging to the organisation. As it is an income it is added to the gross profit figure in the trading/profit and loss account.

After these additional adjustments the new layout of the trading/profit and loss account is shown below.

Trading and profit and loss account of Happy Burgers for year ending 31 December 2007

	£	£	£
Sales			500,000
Less returns inwards			1,000
			499,000
Opening stock		6,000	
Purchases	256,000		
Less returns outwards	500	255,500	
		261,500	
Closing stock		10,000	
Cost of goods sold			251,500
Gross profit			**247,500**
Add discount received			200
			247,700
Less expenses:			
Wages and salaries	55,000		
Add accrual	500	55,500	
Electricity	34,000		
Less prepayment	200	33,800	
Rent and rates		10,000	
Discount allowed		1,000	100,300
Net profit			**147,400**

ACTIVITY 2.2

Trial balance of Trevor Black as at 31 December 2007

	Dr	Cr
	£	£
Debtors	48,650	
Creditors		39,368
Capital		60,000
Bank		2,166
Rent and rates	21,724	
Electricity	4,108	
Telephone	3,390	
Salaries	111,782	
Motor vehicles	44,500	
Office equipment	15,000	
Motor vehicle expenses	21,710	
Drawings	30,550	
Discount allowed	956	
Discount received		1,182
Purchases	277,920	
Sales		514,516
Stock at 1 January 2007	36,942	
	617,232	**617,232**

Notes at 31 December 2007:

- Stock valued at £28,150
- Rates prepaid £500
- Electricity owing £220
- Salaries owing £730

Prepare the trading and profit and loss account of Trevor Black for the year ending 31 December 2007, together with his balance sheet at that date.

ACTIVITY 2.3

Trial balance of Alan Jess as at 31 December 2007

	Dr £	Cr £
Capital		41,864
Purchases	297,000	
Sales		421,800
Repairs to buildings	1,696	
Delivery van	10,000	
Van expenses	3,080	
Land and buildings	170,000	
Loan from bank		100,000
Bank balance	1,080	
Shop fittings	5,120	
Wages and salaries	60,560	
Discounts allowed	270	
Discounts received		2,638
Rates and insurance	5,380	
Debtors	6,350	
Creditors		16,590
Heating and lighting	6,328	
General expenses	4,340	
Sales returns	1,710	
Purchases returns		2,442
Stock at 1 Jan 2007	12,420	
	585,334	**585,334**

Notes at 31 December 2007:

- Stock valued at £15,030
- Rates prepaid £510
- Wages owing £1,120
- Van expenses owing £170

Prepare the trading and profit and loss account of Alan Jess for the year ending 31 December 2007, together with his balance sheet at that date.

☐ DEPRECIATION

Depreciation can be defined as the estimate of the amount of the fall in the value of fixed assets over a stated period of time.

It is important that this is recorded in the organisation's final accounts in order to ensure they give a true reflection of the value of the organisation.

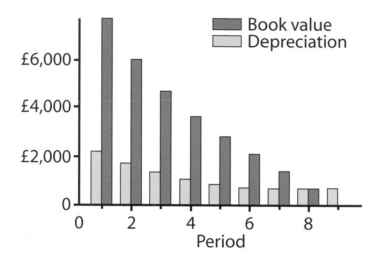

A business's fixed assets will fall in value through time. This fall in value will vary depending on the type of asset. For example, a computer will lose value fairly quickly. Depreciation can be thought of as a cost for using the fixed asset each year.

©iStockphoto.com/maureenpr

Depreciation must be entered in a firm's balance sheet. It is also included with the other operating expenses in the trading/profit and loss account. However, it is important to note that depreciation is a non-cash expense. Although we treat it as such in the trading/profit and loss account, no one is actually *paid* for this expense.

There are various different ways of calculating depreciation and each method will be appropriate to a type of fixed asset. Two of the most common methods are:

- **Straight-line depreciation** – using this method, the value of the asset is reduced by a fixed amount each year. This amount is calculated by taking the cost of the asset, subtracting the scrap value, and then dividing this figure by the asset's estimated life (in years).

  This is the most popular method of calculating depreciation.

- **Declining/reducing balance** – this method writes off a fixed percentage from the value of the asset each year. This means that most of the cost of the asset is charged in the earlier years of its use.

Trading/profit and loss account

As already stated, depreciation for the financial year is included in a firm's trading/profit and loss account as an expense.

Balance sheet

Two new columns are used in the fixed assets section of the balance sheet. In the first column the initial cost of the asset is shown. In the middle column the accumulated depreciation (depreciation to date) is entered. Depreciation to date is calculated by adding the 'provision for depreciation' figure from the trial balance to the depreciation estimated for the current trading period. The provision for depreciation figure represents the depreciation that has been accounted for in previous years, but not this year's depreciation.

Depreciation to date is subtracted from the cost of the fixed asset, to find the net book value of the assets at the end of the accounting period. These net book values are then totalled.

Balance sheet (extract) – fixed assets

	Cost	Depreciation to date	Net book value
	£	£	£
Furniture	6,000	600	5,400
Motor vans	10,000	6,000	4,000
	16,000	**6,600**	**9,400**

As already stated, the two most common methods of calculating depreciation are the straight-line method and the reducing balance method.

We will now examine in more detail how these are calculated.

Trial balance of Happy Burgers (extract)

	Dr	Cr
	£	£
Fixed assets at cost:		
Vehicles	20,000	
Machinery	10,000	
Provision for depreciation		
Vehicles		4,000
Machinery		1,900

Note: In this instance, vehicles are to be depreciated at 10% per annum using the straight-line method and machinery at 10% per annum using the reducing balance method.

The straight-line method

In the trial balance above, the cost of vehicles was £20,000. Vehicles are to be depreciated at 10% per annum using the straight-line method. This method is the easiest to calculate as the depreciation charged is the same each year – annual depreciation is a fixed percentage of the cost of the asset.

©iStockphoto.com/gocosmonaut

In this case it is 10% of £20,000, which is £2,000 per year. This £2,000 is included in the trading/profit and loss account along with the other operating expenses, as illustrated below.

Trading/profit and loss account of Happy Burgers for year ending 31 December 2007

	£	£	£
Sales			500,000
Less returns inwards			1,000
			499,000
Opening stock		6,000	
Purchases	256,000		
Less returns outwards	500	255,500	
		261,500	
Closing stock		10,000	
Cost of goods sold			251,500
Gross profit			**247,500**
Add discount received			200
			247,700
Less expenses:			
Wages and salaries	55,000		
Add accrual	500	55,500	
Electricity	34,000		
Less prepayment	200	33,800	
Rent and rates		10,000	
Discount allowed		1,000	
Depreciation – vehicles		2,000	
Net profit			**145,400**

In the balance sheet under the *depreciation to date* column the £4,000 already provided for is added to this year's depreciation (£2,000).

Balance sheet of Happy Burgers (extract) – fixed assets

	Cost £	Depreciation to date £	Net book value £
Vehicles	20,000	6,000	14,000

The reducing balance method

In the trial balance on page 27, the cost of machinery was £10,000 and the provision for depreciation is £1,900. Machinery is to be depreciated at 10% using the reducing balance method. The calculation of depreciation for this year is slightly more complicated than the straight-line method.

Before the annual depreciation is calculated the net book value of the asset at the beginning of this year must be worked out. In this example

©iStockphoto.com/gprentice

the net book value at the start of the year is £8,100 (£10,000 – £1,900).

The 10% depreciation is then calculated on this value, ie 10% of £8,100 which equals £810.

This £810 is entered in the trading/profit and loss account with the other operating expenses. In the balance sheet the depreciation to date figure is £2,710 (£1,900 + £810) and the net book value is £7,290.

Trading/profit and loss account of Happy Burgers for year ending 31 December 2007

	£	£	£
Sales			500,000
Less returns inwards			1,000
			499,000
Opening stock		6,000	
Purchases	256,000		
Less returns outwards	500	255,500	
		261,500	
Closing stock		10,000	
Cost of goods sold			251,500
Gross profit			**247,500**
Add discount received			200
			247,700
Less expenses:			
Wages and salaries	55,000		
Add accrual	500	55,500	
Electricity	34,000		
Less prepayment	200	33,800	
Rent and rates		10,000	
Discount allowed		1,000	
Depreciation – vehicles		2,000	
Depreciation – machinery		810	103,110
Net profit			**144,590**

Balance sheet of Happy Burgers (extract) – fixed assets

	Cost £	Depreciation to date £	Net book value £
Vehicles	20,000	6,000	14,000
Machinery	10,000	2,710	7,290
	30,000	**8,710**	**21,290**

ACTIVITY 2.4

Trial balance of Kiera O'Hare as at 31 December 2007

	Dr £	Cr £
Bank loan		37,500
Capital		62,500
Purchases and sales	232,500	307,000
Building repairs	4,240	
Motor vehicles at cost	6,000	
Provision for depreciation on motor vehicles		1,200
Motor expenses	1,340	
Land and buildings at cost	50,000	
Bank overdraft		1,000
Furniture and fittings at cost	12,500	
Provision for depreciation on furniture and fittings		1,250
Wages and salaries	43,030	
Discounts	5,305	4,070
Drawings	12,000	
Rates and insurance	3,035	
Debtors and creditors	26,065	20,925
General expenses	7,930	
Stock at 1 January 2007	31,500	
	435,445	**435,445**

Notes at 31 December 2007:

- Stock valued at £44,000
- Wages and salaries owing £1,590
- Rates and insurance prepaid £225
- Motor vehicles to be depreciated at 20% using the straight-line method
- Furniture and fittings to be depreciated at 10% using the straight-line method

Prepare the trading and profit and loss account of Kiera O'Hare for the year ending 31 December 2007, together with her balance sheet at that date.

PROVISION FOR BAD DEBTS

When a business sells its goods to a customer it often needs to allow a period of credit. However, not all debtors will settle the amount that they owe, and some of these debts will become what are known as **bad debts**.

©iStockphoto.com/nickobec

Specific bad debt (bad debts written off)

Sometimes a business is not able to collect a debt. If this is the case, and the business is sure that the debtor will not or cannot pay, the debt will be written off.

Provision (allowance) for bad debts

This can be defined as the estimate by a business of the likely percentage of its debtors which *may* go bad during any one accounting period.

A business cannot be certain about this, but should make an allowance for amounts that may not be paid – the accountant should show prudence (see page 35).

A provision for bad debts is completely different from writing off a bad debt. There should usually be two separate entries in the trading/profit and loss account.

For example, the accountant for Happy Burgers Ltd has advised that from the total debtors figure of £18,000 there are two debtors totalling £300 to be written off, and a provision for bad debts to be created for 5% of debtors to allow for possible future bad debts.

	£
Gross debtors	18,000
Less bad debts written off	300
	17,700
Less provision for bad debts at 5%	885
Net debtors	**16,815**

The tables on pages 32 and 33 show how this would be entered into the trading/profit and loss account, and the balance sheet.

Trading/profit and loss account of Happy Burgers for year ending 31 December 2007

	£	£	£
Sales			500,000
Less returns inwards			1,000
			499,000
Opening stock		6,000	
Purchases	256,000		
Less returns outwards	500	255,500	
		261,500	
Closing stock		10,000	
Cost of goods sold			251,500
Gross profit			**247,500**
Add discount received			200
			247,700
Less expenses:			
Wages and salaries	55,000		
Add accrual	500	55,500	
Electricity	34,000		
Less prepayment	200	33,800	
Rent and rates		10,000	
Discount allowed		1,000	
Depreciation – vehicles		2,000	
Depreciation – machinery		810	
Bad debts written off		300	
Provision for bad debts		885	104,295
Net profit			**143,405**

Balance sheet of Happy Burgers for year ending 31 December 2007

	Cost	Depreciation to date	Net book value
	£	£	£
Fixed assets:			
Vehicles	20,000	6,000	14,000
Machinery	10,000	2,710	7,290
Premises	200,000	0	200,000
	230,000	8,710	221,290
Current assets:			
Stock		10,000	
Debtors	17,700		
Less provision for bad debts	885	16,815	
Bank		10,000	
Cash		2,000	
		38,815	
Less current liabilities:			
Creditors		37,000	
Working capital			1,815
			223,105
Less long-term liabilities:			33,700
Net assets			189,405
Financed by:			
Capital	50,000		
Add net profit	143,405	193,405	
Less drawings		4,000	189,405

Note: If bad debts are already written off, ie they are recorded as bad debts written off in the trial balance, they have already been subtracted from the debtors figure.

Generally, bad debts written off should be included as an operating expense in the trading/profit and loss account. If the specific bad debt was in the trial balance, it will not affect the balance sheet. However, if you are instructed, for example, to write off £200 of bad debts from the debtors figure, the balance sheet will be affected.

Increases/decreases in provision for bad debts

Once a provision for bad debts has been created the amount of the provision must be reviewed each year.

If it is decided that the size of the provision needs to be increased then the amount of the increase is charged to the profit and loss account as an expense and it is recorded as an increase in the provision for bad debts. However, the full provision is deducted from the debtors figure in the balance sheet.

If the provision for bad debts is to be reduced the difference is added to the profit and loss account as a reduction in the provision for bad debts. Again, it is the full provision that is deducted from the debtors figure in the balance sheet.

Rules

An increase in the provision for bad debts

Trading/profit and loss account – list the increase with the operating expenses.
Balance sheet – deduct the provision from the debtors account.

A decrease in the provision for bad debts

Trading/profit and loss account – treat the decrease as income and add it to gross profit, just like discount received.

Balance sheet – subtract the decrease from the provision for bad debts.

ACTIVITY 2.5

Trial balance of Tom Hegarty as at 31 December 2007 (first year of trading)

	Dr £	Cr £
Sales		36,050
Purchases	5,580	
Wages	6,000	
Rent	9,000	
Insurance	3,700	
Electricity	920	
Advertising	1,930	
Telephone	725	
Administration expenses	625	
Rental income		750
Equipment	7,500	
Debtors	600	
Creditors		810
Bank	530	
Capital		7,500
Drawings	8,000	
	45,110	**45,110**

Notes at 31 December 2007:

- Stock valued at £395
- Advertising prepaid £130
- Equipment to be depreciated at 25% using the straight-line method
- Accruals – administration £80, telephone £145, electricity £270
- Provision for bad debts of 20% of debtors to be made

Prepare the trading and profit and loss account of Tom Hegarty for the year ending 31 December 2007.

Accounting concepts

Imagine a situation where a business owner takes copies of its financial records to six different accountants and asks each one to calculate its profit for the year. Two weeks later each accountant provides their figures. There are six different profit figures, with very wide variations between them. If this happened, what impression would people have of the accounting profession?

©iStockphoto.com/DNY59

To prevent this happening, various rules or accepted ways of doing things have been developed. These rules are known as *concepts* and *conventions* (for our purposes there is no effective difference between a concept and a convention, so we shall refer to them as concepts). In addition, it has been necessary to draw up further rules. These are known as **Statements of Standard Accounting Practice (SSAPs)** and, more recently, **Financial Reporting Standards (FRSs)**.

Together, all of these concepts and statements bring about *consistency* within accounting. This is very important, both for the *credibility* of the accountants, and for the *reliability* of the financial results that they report.

You will already have used some of the concepts when preparing the final accounts. For example, the business entity concept states that only the assets and liabilities of the business are included in the final accounts; the personal assets of the owner(s) should not be included.

☐ BUSINESS ENTITY CONCEPT

The financial reports of the business show only the assets and liabilities of the business. If the owner of a business also owned a small boat for personal use, the boat would not appear as a fixed asset in the business's balance sheet. This is because the boat is a personal asset of the owner, and the owner is a separate entity from the business entity.

☐ PRUDENCE CONCEPT

The accountant is responsible for ensuring that the business's books are an accurate representation of the business's 'health'. This means ensuring that the assets are not overvalued. In order to do this, accountants are advised to be *conservative* in their judgements. This is known as the concept of prudence.

The prudence concept is also relevant when calculating profit. The accountant tends to understate profit – for example, making an allowance for bad debts.

☐ GOING CONCERN CONCEPT

What do you understand by the term 'going concern'?

It is assumed that the business will continue to operate in the future. Imagine a building is valued at £100,000. The accountant would continue to show its cost in the balance sheet. The only time the accountant would record it at its resale value is if the business was going to close down in the near future. In this case, the balance sheet would look very different, as the value of fixed assets would be much lower.

☐ MATERIALITY CONCEPT

Although accountancy is concerned with charging expenses to the right period, this rule only applies to items that have 'material' value. For example, an accountant will not be concerned with ensuring the right numbers of paperclips are charged to each month – they will charge the box of paperclips because it is a small item.

☐ MATCHING CONCEPT

Accountants match expenses to the period they belong to. For example, all electricity bills should be included in the final accounts for any year. If a business knows that it won't receive December's bill until January of the next year, the business needs to estimate how much the bill will be and add it to the operating expenses.

ACTIVITY 2.6

What best illustrates the matching concept?

☐ OBJECTIVITY CONCEPT

The final accounts should not reflect the personal expectations of the owners of the business. The accounts must be unbiased, ie the information should be objective.

ACTIVITY 2.7

Can you provide examples of objective (unbiased) and subjective (biased) reporting?

☐ MONEY MEASUREMENT CONCEPT

This concept requires that all information must be stated in financial or monetary terms. The reason for this is to permit easy comparison of figures.

☐ SSAPs AND FRSs

A SSAP is a document prepared by the Accounting Standards Board (ASB). All accountants are bound to abide by their terms. SSAPs are no longer issued, but those that are still current come under the control of the ASB. A number of SSAPs have been replaced with FRSs in an attempt to reduce the number of accounting treatments.

Some of the main SSAPs and FRSs are:

- SSAP2 Disclosure of accounting policies
- SSAP5 Accounting for value-added tax (VAT)
- SSAP9 Stocks and long-term contracts
- FRS15 Tangible fixed assets
- FRS18 accounting policies

REVISION QUESTION

Explain what a trial balance is and its purpose.

CHAPTER 3

Ratio analysis

There are many users of financial information, and although the needs of these users may differ they all share a need for information that is easy to understand. Some of these users are:

- Management
- Employees
- Owners
- Investors
- Lenders
- Suppliers
- Customers
- Customs and Excise
- Inland Revenue
- The Registrar of Companies
- Journalists
- Researchers
- Competitors/rivals
- Industry associations

©iStockphoto.com/lisegagne

ACTIVITY 3.1

What type of financial information might each of these users want and why might they need it?

Each of these users is interested in the financial information for different reasons. Examples are given below.

©iStockphoto.com/aldomurillo

☐ MANAGEMENT

- Management will want to know if the business is profitable.
- Management will want to know if the business can pay expenses on time.

☐ EMPLOYEES

- Employees may be interested in the firm's profitability, as some receive a share of company profits.
- The 1994 EU Works Council Directive gives employees in certain multinational corporations (MNCs) the right to set up works councils that must be consulted by management.

☐ OWNERS

- Owners will want to know if management is making good use of the business's resources.

☐ INVESTORS

- Investors will want to know what profit is being made.
- They will also want to know if the level of return on their investment is comparable with other investment opportunities.

☐ LENDERS

- Lenders will want to know if the firm has the ability to make loan repayments.
- They will also want to know how quickly the organisation can repay its loans. The answers to these decisions may influence the rate of interest to charge.

©iStockphoto.com/marmion

☐ SUPPLIERS

- Suppliers will want to know if an organisation can pay its invoices on time.
- They will also be interested in the firm's liquidity and its cash flow.
- Suppliers may also be interested in the business's long-term plans.

☐ CUSTOMERS

- Customers will want to know if the business is stable. For example, a conference organiser would need to have confidence in the business before paying over a large deposit.

☐ INLAND REVENUE AND CUSTOMS AND EXCISE

- Companies must pay corporate tax on profits made, and must charge VAT on the goods and services they sell. The Inland Revenue and Customs and Excise will therefore need to ensure that the correct amounts are paid, based on the firm's financial figures.

☐ THE REGISTRAR OF COMPANIES

- All companies must send a copy of their accounts to the Registrar of Companies.

☐ COMPETITORS

There are different reasons that competitors may be interested in a firm's financial figures. They will want answers to the following questions:

- Are the firm's sales increasing or decreasing?
- Are certain departments doing well?
- What is the average price charged?
- What is the average amount spent by customers?

Ratios can help to measure company performance. There are four main groups of ratios, which look at *profitability, liquidity, working capital management* and *investment appraisal*. Ratios are useful as they express financial data in simpler formats, such as percentages, and allow comparisons to be made.

There are various ways that these comparisons can be made:

- Ratios can be compared to ratios of past years to analyse performance.
- Ratios can be compared to the **budget** to examine if the business is performing as expected.
- Ratios can be compared to ratios from other businesses in the same industry to analyse how the firm has performed in relation to competitors.
- Ratios can be compared to standards recommended by interested organisations, for example a bank.

Profitability ratios

One way of assessing the performance of a company is to look at its profitability in relation to its sales.

☐ GROSS PROFIT MARGIN RATIO

The **gross profit margin ratio** is found by expressing the gross profit as a percentage of sales ...

gross profit margin % = (gross profit/sales) × 100%

The gross profit margin ratio tells us the profit a business makes on its cost of sales, or cost of goods sold. Gross profit is the profit earned before expenses are deducted, so the gross profit margin should be higher than the net profit margin.

The gross profit margin is influenced by many factors including a change in the level of sales and/or a change in the cost of goods sold.

The gross profit margin allows the financial user to examine the relationship between gross profit and sales. For example, if the gross profit margin is 60% this means that the organisation is making 60p worth of gross profit for every £1 worth of sales.

Note: within the context of limited company accounts, the equivalent profit figure that may be used to calculate this ratio is the 'operating profit' figure.

Question: Why might the cost of goods sold rise?

Answer: Suppliers' prices might increase.
There might be a change in the sales mix.

The table below shows a few examples of the gross profit margins from different businesses.

	Leisure & hotels	International airline	Manufacturer	Retailer	Discount airline	Refining	Pizza restaurants	Accounting software
Gross profit margin	9.64%	5.62%	35.14%	11.41%	27.46%	11.99%	47.52%	89.55%

As you can see, the gross profit margins vary from business to business and from industry to industry. For example, the international airline has a typical gross profit margin of only 5.62% yet the accounting software business has a typical gross profit margin of 89.55%.

If a company's raw materials go up a lot, the gross profit margin will go down unless the business increases its selling prices at the same time.

NET PROFIT MARGIN RATIO

The **net profit margin ratio** is calculated by subtracting expenses from gross profit. The net profit margin is found by expressing the net profit as a percentage of sales.

net profit % = (net profit/sales) × 100% or (profit before interest and taxation/sales) × 100%

There are two versions of this ratio – one for net profit and the other for profit before interest and taxation. In some cases only the term 'net profit' is used, and in other cases, especially published accounts, 'profit before interest and taxation' is used.

The net profit margin tells us the amount of net profit per £1 of sales a business has earned. That is, after taking account of the cost of sales, the administration costs, the selling and distribution costs, and all other expenses, the net profit is the profit that is left, out of which the business will pay interest, tax, dividends, and so on.

The table below shows the net profit margins of the businesses in the table at the top of the page.

	Leisure & hotels	International airline	Manufacturer	Retailer	Discount airline	Refining	Pizza restaurants	Accounting software
Net profit margin	7.36%	4.05%	−10.48%	1.63%	10.87%	12.63%	7.55%	27.15%

Just like the gross profit margins, the net profit margins also vary from business to business and from industry to industry. When we compare the gross and the net profit margins we can gain a good impression of non-production and non-direct costs such as administration, marketing and finance.

The tables show that the international airline's gross profit margin is the lowest of the group of eight businesses at only 5.62%, but its net profit margin is 4.05% – only a little lower than its gross profit margin. On the other hand, the discount airline's gross profit margin is 27.46% but its net profit margin is a lot less than that at 10.87%. This means that the discount airline's expenses as a percentage of sales is higher than for the international airlines. As already stated, these comparisons provide a great insight into the cost structure of these businesses.

The software business has a very high gross profit margin of 89.55% but a net profit margin of 27.15%. This is still high, but it is obvious that the administration and similar expenses are very high while its cost of sales and operating costs are relatively very low.

Individual expenses can also be looked at by using the following formula ...

specific expenses/sales × 100%

This will show if an individual expense has changed in proportion to sales. If sales increased we would expect some expenses to also increase, but we would hope that the increase was in line with the sales increase.

ROCE (RETURN ON CAPITAL EMPLOYED)

ROCE is found by expressing the net profit as a percentage of the total capital employed in the business ...

ROCE% = (net profit/capital employed) × 100%

©iStockphoto.com/Duncan Walker

ROCE shows the profitability of the business in relation to the size of capital employed. Most owners would hope that this percentage would compare favourably with other investment opportunities.

In accounting, there can be different definitions of certain terms, and so the term 'capital employed' can mean different things. It can, for example, include bank loans and overdrafts since these are funds employed within the firm. As there are different interpretations of what ROCE can mean, there are variations in the formula used.

Definitions of capital employed
Capital employed = total assets
Capital employed = fixed assets + current assets – current liabilities
Capital employed = ordinary share capital + reserves + preference share capital + minority interest + provisions + total borrowings – intangible assets
Trading capital employed = share capital + reserves + all borrowings including lease obligations, overdraft, minority interest, provisions, associates and investments
Overall capital employed = share capital + reserves + all borrowings including lease obligations, overdraft, minority interest and provisions
Capital employed = total fixed assets + current assets – (current liabilities + long-term liabilities + provisions)
Capital employed = fixed assets + current assets – (creditors + provisions)

Although there are many definitions, as it is the most common, the following definition should be used.

capital employed = long-term loan + share capital + reserves

☐ FIXED ASSET TURNOVER

Fixed asset turnover is found by ...

sales/fixed assets

This ratio measures how effectively the business uses its fixed assets to generate sales. The ratio shows how much sales are generated with every £1 worth of fixed assets.

Investment ratios

☐ GEARING RATIO

Gearing (or as it is also called, **leverage**) expresses the relationship between a firm's long term debt and its capital employed. It is found by ...

(long term debt/capital employed) × 100%

(long-term debt = loans + preference shares
capital employed = ordinary share capital + reserves)

Gearing is concerned with the relationship between a business's long-term liabilities and its capital employed. The idea is that this relationship ought to have a suitable balance, with the shareholders' funds being significantly larger than the long-term liabilities.

Shareholders like this relationship to be in their favour because:

- Ordinary shares earn dividends, but in poor years dividends may be zero, ie businesses don't always need to pay dividends out.
- Long-term liabilities are usually in the form of loans and interest has to be paid, even in bad years.
- Ordinary shareholders have the voting rights at general meetings and can make significant decisions.
- Long-term liability holders don't have any voting rights at general meetings, but they have the power to override the wishes of the shareholders if there are severe problems over their interest or capital repayments.

☐ EARNINGS PER SHARE (EPS)

EPS expresses the relationship between the profit available to ordinary shareholders and the number of ordinary shares. It is found by ...

profit available to ordinary shareholders /number of ordinary shares

This ratio shows the amount each share is earning for the investor.

DIVIDEND PER SHARE (DPS)

DPS is found by dividing the firm's dividends by the number of ordinary shares ...

dividends/number of ordinary shares

This ratio measures the dividend paid out per share. It shows the amount of money ordinary shareholders actually receive. This is not the same as EPS as it shows only the dividend paid to shareholders. The earnings of the company are also made up of retained profits.

©iStockphoto.com/Stefan Klein

Liquidity (Efficiency) ratios

Liquidity refers to the ability of the business to meet current obligations. All businesses will need a minimum amount of **working capital** (current assets – current liabilities) although there is no legal requirement as to what size this should be.

The balance sheet is used to calculate ratios that measure the ability of the business to pay liabilities from current assets.

CURRENT (WORKING CAPITAL) RATIO

The current ratio is found by dividing the firm's current assets by its current liabilities ...

current assets/current liabilities = x:1

This balance between current assets and current liabilities is expressed in the form of a ratio. For example, a business with current assets of £100,000 and current liabilities of £50,000 has a current ratio of:

100,000/50,000 = 2 :1

Although different businesses will have different acceptable ratios, as a rule of thumb a ratio of 2:1 is considered to be good. This means that the business has £2 worth of current assets for every £1 worth of current liabilities.

If the ratio is any lower, the business may find it difficult to meet its current liabilities. Conversely, a higher ratio may mean that although current liabilities should be met, the business may be holding too much current assets. For example, it may have too much cash (which is non-interest bearing), stock levels may be too high (which is costly), debtors may be too high (which could be risky), or creditors may be too low (the business may not be taking full advantage of credit facilities).

☐ ACID TEST (QUICK RATIO)

The **acid test ratio** is found by deducting stock from the current assets before dividing the result by current liabilities ...

(current assets – stock)/current liabilities = x:1

This ratio deducts stock from the current assets figure. This is because stock is the least liquid asset (ie the hardest to turn into cash). This means that the firm is left with assets that can readily be turned into cash if it needs to meet its current liabilities. The rule of thumb for this ratio is 1:1, meaning that the firm has £1 worth of liquid assets for every £1 worth of current assets.

If the ratio is any lower, the business may find it difficult to meet its current liabilities. Conversely, a higher ratio may mean that although current liabilities should be met, the business may be holding too much current assets. For example, it may have too much cash (which is non-interest bearing), debtors may be too high (which could be risky), or creditors may be too low (the business may not be taking full advantage of credit facilities).

©iStockphoto.com/kevinj

☐ STOCK TURNOVER

A problem faced by most businesses is getting a balance between holding too much stock and holding too little.

Holding too much stock has various disadvantages, for example:

- Cash has to be paid out early which might be put to better use.
- Stock may deteriorate or become obsolete.
- Space will be required to hold the stock which will be costly.

On the other hand, holding too little stock also has disadvantages, for example:

- Sales may be lost if orders cannot be met.
- A lack of stock can halt the entire production process for some businesses.

Stock turnover is the number of days that stock is held on average and is found by dividing the average stock by the cost of goods sold and multiplying the result by 365 (one year) ...

(average stock /cost of goods sold) x 365 = stock turnover (days)

(cost of goods sold = opening stock + purchases – closing stock)

This measures the average number of days per financial year that stock is held by the business.

Alternatively, stock turnover may be calculated by dividing the cost of goods sold by the average stock ...

cost of goods sold/average stock *(cost of goods sold = opening stock + purchases – closing stock)*

This measures the number of times stock turns over each year.

Stock turnover will vary between businesses. For example, an organisation dealing with fresh produce would have a significantly higher stock turnover than an engineering business.

☐ AVERAGE DEBTORS COLLECTION PERIOD

This calculation shows the average length of time in days that it takes debtors to pay their invoices. For most businesses a figure of 30 days would be acceptable but this will depend on the nature of the business. For example, an engineering firm would be likely to have a much higher figure than this.

The average debtor collection period is found by ...

(debtors/credit sales) × 365

©iStockphoto.com/hillwoman2

One way that a firm can improve debtor payments is to offer cash discounts if invoices are paid within a stipulated time period.

☐ AVERAGE CREDITORS REPAYMENT PERIOD

This calculation shows the average length of time in days that it takes the business to pay its invoices. For most businesses a figure of 30 days would be acceptable but this will depend on the nature of the business.

The average creditor payment period is found by ...

(creditors/credit purchases) × 365

Non–financial measures

Company performance can also be measured by non-financial measures. Examples of these might include:

- Customer satisfaction/service quality
- Employee satisfaction surveys
- Staff appraisal systems
- Innovation reviews

Limitations of ratios

Despite the advantages of ratio analysis, there are some limitations which users should be aware of when they are making judgements about an organisation:

- Ratios are based on *past performance* which means they may not represent what will actually happen in the future.
- Different companies have *different accounting policies*. This means it may be difficult to make comparisons between companies.
- Different countries have *different rules*. United States (US) accounts and German accounts are prepared differently which will also result in difficulties if comparisons are to be made on an international basis.
- *Inflation* is a consideration – if there are price rises this can distort the figures.
- *Industry standards* may not be the best benchmark to assess performance.
- Financial ratios ignore *other objectives* of the company.

ACTIVITY 3.2

1. You are required to analyse the financial statements below using the following ratios, and comment on the strengths and weaknesses of the figures.

   (a) ROCE
   (b) Gross profit percentage/margin
   (c) Net profit percentage/margin
   (d) Current ratio

   (e) Acid test ratio
   (f) Debtor collection period (days)
   (g) Creditor payment period (days)
   (h) Stock turnover (days)

   Extracts from the figures for the last two years' trading are as follows.

	2006 £	2007 £
Sales	480,000	800,000
Cost of sales	320,000	600,000
Purchases	320,000	636,000
Gross profit	160,000	200,000
Net profit	120,000	140,000
Fixed assets	140,000	150,000
Stock	28,000	64,000
Debtors	40,000	80,000
Bank (not overdraft)	40,000	80,000
Creditors	40,000	80,000
Long-term bank loan	40,000	40,000
Share capital and reserves	140,000	180,000

2. Study the following extracts from the financial statements of two similar types of travel agency.

	2006 £	2007 £
Sales	120,000	180,000
Opening stock	36,000	33,500
Closing stock	24,000	27,500
Gross profit	30,000	36,000
Net profit	15,000	24,000
Fixed assets	200,000	140,000
Current assets	50,000	40,000
Current liabilities	5,000	10,000
Net assets	42,000	44,000
Capital	42,000	41,000

Analyse the profitability, liquidity and efficiency of the two businesses. Your calculations should be accompanied by a detailed memo explaining your findings.

REVISION QUESTION

You have been given the following information from the accounts of Siobhán Connelly.

	£
Sales	130,000
Cost of sales	25,400
Purchases	65,600
Closing stock	21,000
Gross profit	60,000
Expenses	23,000
Net profit	37,000
Fixed assets	50,490
Total current assets	63,420
Current liabilities	48,210
Working capital	15,210
Bank loan	40,000
Capital employed as at 1 Jan 07	5,280
Net profit	37,000
Drawings	16,580
Capital employed as at 31 Dec 07	25,700

(a) An accountant has worked out the following ratios for Mugs Ltd for the year 2007. You are asked to calculate the same ratios to two decimal places for Siobhán Connelly.

Mugs Ltd

Gross profit percentage/margin	30%
Net profit percentage/margin	21%
Current ratio	2.1:1
ROCE	6.3%
Acid test ratio	0.9:1
Fixed asset turnover	6 times
Gearing	85%
Stock turnover times	5.8 times

(b) Identify the liquidity ratios and explain the significance of these results in relation to the results for Mugs Ltd.

(c) Identify the profitability ratios and compare the results for Mugs Ltd with Siobhán Connelly's results.

(d) Identify the performance ratios and comment on the results. Suggest reasons why these ratios may be different for the two businesses.

(e) Explain the purpose of the gearing ratio and its significance to both businesses.

(f) Explain why a firm should not rely solely on ratios as a decision-making device.

PAST PAPER QUESTIONS

1. Dave is a wealthy businessman with business interests throughout Northern Ireland. He is considering an investment of up to £100,000 in Internet NI Ltd, a locally based business which provides internet services. The business has been established for one year and Dave feels that it could benefit from further investment.

Matt, the manager of Internet NI Ltd, supplied Dave with the financial statements. At first glance they appeared very promising to Dave. Internet NI Ltd reported a net profit before tax of £25,000 for the first year of operations. Matt claimed that this was not a particularly good result due to start-up costs incurred in an area of high unemployment.

Dave examined the financial statements in more detail, calculating some important financial ratios for the business. The results, shown in Table 1 below, gave him a better insight into the financial affairs of the business, particularly the profitability and liquidity of Internet NI Ltd. Dave thought that further investigation was required before deciding whether or not to invest in the business.

Table 1: Financial ratios relating to Internet NI Ltd

Financial ratio	2005
Return on capital employed	25%
Gross profit percentage	50%
Net profit percentage	10%
Current ratio	0.8:1
Acid test ratio	0.75:1
Fixed asset turnover	7 times

(a) Explain why the reported profit for the year is not necessarily the same as the closing cash balance. [4]

(b) Using the following ratios, explain the importance of Internet NI Ltd, as outlined in Table 1.
   (i) The return on capital employed ratio ((net profit/capital employed) × 100%) [3]
   (ii) The gross profit percentage ((gross profit/sales) × 100%) [3]
   (iii) The net profit percentage ((net profit/sales) × 100% [3]
   (iv) The current ratio (current assets/current liabilities) [3]
   (v) The acid test ratio ((current assets – stock)/current liabilities) [3]
   (vi) The fixed asset turnover ratio (sales/fixed assets) [3]

(c) Evaluate the potential advantages and drawbacks to Dave of using financial ratios when deciding whether to invest in Internet NI Ltd. [12]

PAST PAPER ANSWERS

1. (a) Reported profit will not necessarily be the same as closing cash balance for the accounting period due to timing differences, accounting adjustments and non-cash expenses recorded in trading/profit and loss account for the period (eg adjustments for closing stocks, accruals and prepayments, and depreciation expenses). Other examples include:

    • Capital expenditure not recorded in profit and loss a/c
    • Investment/reinvestment
    • Additional sources of finance, ie loans, shares, increases in cash
    • Retained profits/reserves   [4]

    Level 1: ([1])

    Knowledge and understanding of concepts of cash flow and profits is demonstrated but this is limited. Application of this knowledge to the question context, if present, is very limited. Quality of written communication is limited.

    Level 2: ([2]–[3])

    Adequate knowledge and understanding of concepts of cash flow and profits is demonstrated. There is some application of this knowledge to the question context. Quality of written communication is satisfactory.

    Level 3: ([4])

    Thorough knowledge and understanding of concepts of cash flow and profits is demonstrated. There is good application of knowledge to the question context. Quality of written communication is of a high standard.

   (b) Note: In parts i–vi, relevant points/valid alternative suggestions will be accepted.

    (i) The return on capital employed ratio = (net profit/capital employed) × 100%

    A value of 25% appears to be a reasonable level of return on the investment, compared to alternatives such as interest on a bank account. It is not necessarily a problem, although it is dependent upon the level of capital invested. The £100,000 quoted appears reasonable in context, suggesting that the profit before tax is confirmed at £25,000. To properly appreciate this ratio, we would need to know how it is forecasted to change over time and its value compared to similar businesses.   [3]

    (ii) The gross profit percentage = (gross profit/sales) × 100%

    The company is making a 50% margin on sales turnover, which would be expected since an internet service provider is unlikely to carry stock or have large amounts of purchases, being service-orientated. This appears a reasonable level of return given the demand for services. It would need to be compared with similar businesses or an industry average/ standard, in addition to examination into the future.   [3]

    (iii) The net profit percentage = (net profit/sales) × 100%

    The company is making a 10% margin on sales turnover, which may be considered reasonable, since it appears to be a start-up company and may need time to improve margins due to higher levels of expenses in the initial phase. Given the suggestion of the poor performance of this particular business, it is important to be aware of the potential trend over time. However, it is considerably lower than the net profit margin, suggesting a high level of overheads in the business which would need additional scrutiny.   [3]

    (iv) The current ratio = current assets/current liabilities

    A value of 0.8:1 is lower than the recommended benchmark of 2:1. This could be a problem if it continues, since it indicates the inability of the company to meet its debts. It could be indicative of the nature of the company, since internet service companies are unlikely to hold high levels of stocks, but rather incur high debtors levels or experience cash flow problems perhaps due to the nature of project/systems work. To properly evaluate this ratio, we would need additional information regarding the make-up of current assets and monitored over time. [3]

(v) The acid test ratio = (current assets – stock)/current liabilities

A value of 0.75:1 is lower than the recommended benchmark of 1:1. This could be a problem if it continues, since it indicates the inability of the company to meet its debts. It could be indicative of the nature of the company, since internet service companies are unlikely to hold high levels of stocks, but rather incur high debtors levels or experience cash flow problems perhaps due to the nature of project/systems work. In addition, it has changed little from the current ratio value, suggesting that the problems lie in debtors control and cash flow problems. To properly evaluate this ratio, we would need additional information regarding the make-up of current assets and monitored over time. [3]

(vi) The fixed asset turnover ratio = sales/fixed assets

A value of seven times appears reasonable. This indicates that the company generates sales revenues seven times the value of the total assets, suggesting that the company is efficient in the use of assets. This would be indicative of internet service companies, in that it is unlikely that they would hold huge levels of fixed assets, and generate revenues from a small asset base and consultancy activities. To properly evaluate this ratio, we would need additional information regarding the assets and monitored over time. [3]

[18]

Level 1: ([1]–[6])

Some knowledge and understanding of ratios is demonstrated but this is limited. Application of this knowledge to the question context, if present, is very limited. Quality of written communication is limited.

Level 2: ([7]–[12])

Adequate knowledge and understanding of ratios is demonstrated. There is some application of this knowledge to the question context. Quality of written communication is satisfactory.

Level 3: ([13]–[18])

Thorough knowledge and understanding of ratios is demonstrated. There is good application of knowledge to the question context. Quality of written communication is of a high standard.

(c) Potential advantages of using financial ratios:

- They give Dave an indication that there may be problems concerning liquidity and profitability.
- Quantitative measures facilitate assessment of the financial performance of the business across a range of areas.
- Comparisons can be made regarding financial performance over time.
- Comparisons can be made regarding financial performance relative to other businesses, and other investments.
- Financial ratios can be used in addition to variance analysis to evaluate attainment of performance targets.

Potential drawbacks of using financial ratios:

- It may be difficult to make comparisons with similar businesses due to different accounting policies.
- Ratios are only as accurate as the underlying information in financial statements, and thus are subject to manipulation and seasonal factors.

- Analysis is limited to quantitative issues, providing little information regarding rivals, etc.
- This ignores qualitative issues in the broader business environment and non-financial indicators, eg goodwill, reputation, quality, and staff turnover/wider economic indicators.
- Ratio analysis may not apply/be relevant in certain circumstances. [12]

Level 1: ([1]–[4])

Some knowledge and understanding of potential advantages and drawbacks of using financial ratios is demonstrated but this is limited. Up to two points accepted (one advantage and one drawback). Application of this knowledge to the question context, if present, is very limited. Quality of written communication is limited.

Level 2: ([5]–[8])

Adequate knowledge and understanding of potential advantages and drawbacks of using financial ratios is demonstrated. Up to four points accepted (ideally two advantages and two drawbacks). There is some application of this knowledge to the question context. Quality of written communication is satisfactory.

Level 3: ([9]–[12])

Thorough knowledge and understanding of potential advantages and drawbacks of using financial ratios is demonstrated. Up to six points accepted (ideally three advantages and three drawbacks). There is good application of knowledge to the question context. Quality of written communication is of a high standard.

Note: Answers must include a balanced approach in terms of arguments forwarded.

PAST PAPER QUESTIONS

2. Study the information below and answer the questions that follow.

The Viridian Group plc was established in February 1998, and has business interests in the purchase, transmission, distribution and supply of electricity in Northern Ireland (NI). This company in turn owns Northern Ireland Electricity (NIE). However, neither it nor NIE is actually engaged in the generation of electricity – this is the responsibility of individual power stations within NI (eg Premier Power) and other electricity suppliers in Great Britain.

The electricity regulator 'Ofreg' has the power to regulate tariffs levied in relation to the electricity supplied to customers of NIE. The aim in this instance is to safeguard the interests of consumers in NI against excessive profit-taking by NIE, which in turn limits the growth potential (in terms of sales revenues and profits) of this business sector.

The Viridian Group plc is also engaged in a range of 'unregulated' business activities. Indeed, during the year 2003, the group sold various assets including the 'Moyle Interconnector' (an electricity connector between NI and Scotland), 'Fleet Solutions', and 'Lislyn' (private limited companies within their ownership). During 2004, the group expressed an interest in building an 'Ireland–Wales' electricity connector.

The Viridian Group plc is quoted on the London and Dublin stock exchanges, enabling investors to trade in the company's shares. Financial data in respect of the financial years 2003 and 2004 is summarised in Table 1.

Table 1: Summary financial data

Financial year ended:	31 March 2003	31 March 2004
	£m	£m
Sales	781.2	834.2
Profit before tax (operating profit)	78.4	89.2
Dividends	43.2	44.8
Fixed assets	1089.0	967.8
Current assets	226.4	231.6
Current liabilities	284.9	244.7
Long-term debt	622.0	550.4
Share capital	33.3	33.3
Reserves	213.7	243.7
Capital employed	247.0	277.0

The Viridian Group plc has an issued share capital of 133,015,906 ordinary 25p shares. Any opinion expressed by investment analysts states that the Viridian Group plc operates in a "very regulated and mature industry with limited growth potential".

(Adapted from (i) Stock Market Annual 2005 (p122) and (ii) Stock Market Annual 2004 (p65), published by Private Research, Dalkey, Dublin, Ireland)

(a) You are required to one decimal place calculate the following accounting ratios, using the formulae provided:

(i) **Return on capital employed:**

return on capital employed = (net profit before tax/capital employed) × 100%

2003   **2004**

$$\frac{\qquad}{\qquad} \times 100\% \qquad \frac{\qquad}{\qquad} \times 100\%$$

Return on capital employed: ☐ %   ☐ %   [2]

(ii) **Net profit margin:**

net profit margin = (profit before tax/sales) × 100%

2003   **2004**

$$\frac{\qquad}{\qquad} \times 100\% \qquad \frac{\qquad}{\qquad} \times 100\%$$

Net profit margin: ☐ %   ☐ %   [2]

(iii) **Fixed asset turnover:**

fixed asset turnover = sales/fixed assets

	2003	2004

Fixed asset turnover: ☐ times   ☐ times   [2]

(iv) **Current ratio:**

current ratio = current assets/current liabilities

	2003	2004

Current ratio: ☐ times   ☐ times   [2]

(v) **Gearing:**

gearing = (long-term debt/capital employed) × 100%

	2003	2004

× 100%   × 100%

Gearing: ☐ %   ☐ %   [2]

(b) Using the information above and the ratios calculated in part (a), discuss the financial position of the Viridian Group plc with respect to the following ratios:

(i) The return on capital employed ratio [3]

(ii) The net profit margin [3]

(iii) The fixed asset turnover ratio [3]

(iv) The current ratio [3]

(v) The gearing ratio [3]

(c) Evaluate the usefulness of ratio analysis to analyse the final accounts of a company such as Viridian Group plc. [16]

PAST PAPER ANSWERS

2. (a) (i) **Return on capital employed:**

		2003		2004	
$\dfrac{\text{profit before tax}}{\text{capital employed}} \times 100\%$		$\dfrac{78.4}{247.0} \times 100\%$		$\dfrac{89.2}{277.0} \times 100\%$	
Return on capital employed:		**31.7%**		**32.2%**	[2]

(ii) **Net profit margin:**

		2003		2004	
$\dfrac{\text{profit before tax}}{\text{sales}} \times 100\%$		$\dfrac{78.4}{781.2} \times 100\%$		$\dfrac{89.2}{834.2} \times 100\%$	
Net profit margin:		**10.0%**		**10.7%**	[2]

(iii) **Fixed asset turnover:**

	2003	2004	
$\dfrac{\text{sales}}{\text{fixed assets}}$	$\dfrac{781.2}{1089.0}$	$\dfrac{834.2}{967.8}$	
Fixed asset turnover:	**0.7** times	**0.9** times	[2]

(iv) **Current ratio:**

	2003	2004	
$\dfrac{\text{current assets}}{\text{current liabilities}}$	$\dfrac{226.4}{284.9}$	$\dfrac{231.6}{244.7}$	
Current ratio:	**0.8** times	**0.9** times	[2]

(v) **Gearing:**

		2003		2004	
$\dfrac{\text{long-term debt}}{\text{capital employed}} \times 100\%$		$\dfrac{622.0}{247.0} \times 100\%$		$\dfrac{550.0}{277.0} \times 100\%$	
Gearing:		**251.8%**		**198.6%**	[2]

([1] for correct calculation of each ratio; [1]×10) [10]

(b) (i) **The return on capital employed ratio: 31.7% (2003); 32.2% (2004)**

A value of 32.2% (2004) appears to be a reasonable level of return on the investment, compared to 31.7% (2003) and alternatives such as interest on a bank account. It is not necessarily a problem, although it is dependent upon the level of capital invested. The amounts quoted appear reasonable in context, suggesting that both the profit and asset base are dominant factors, since the investment in fixed assets declined over the two-year period yet profitability increased marginally. [3]

(ii) **The net profit margin: 10.0% (2003); 10.7% (2004)**

A value of 10.7% (2004) appears to be a reasonable level of return on the sales revenues generated from operations, compared to 10.0% (2003). It is not necessarily a problem, although it is dependent upon the level of operational expenses. The amounts quoted appear reasonable in context, suggesting that the cost control may be an issue, since the business activities may require continuous support and high maintenance of the network/electricity grid. Profit is the dominant factor in this business, since the investment in fixed assets declined over the two-year period, yet profitability increased marginally. Factors which appear to impact the revenue streams, and ultimately the profitability of the company, are sales revenues and cost levels. [3]

(iii) **Fixed asset turnover: 0.72 times (2003); 0.86 times (2004)**

A value of 0.86 times (2004) appears low. This indicates that the company generates sales revenues 0.86 times the value of the fixed assets, suggesting that the company is marginally efficient in the use of assets, although it does improve year-on-year. This would be indicative of utility/service companies, in that it is likely they would hold huge levels of fixed assets and generate revenues from a large fixed asset base, ie the electricity grid/network. To properly evaluate this issue, we would need additional information regarding the fixed assets. [3]

(iv) **The current ratio: 0.79 times (2003); 0.95 times (2004)**

A value of 0.95:1 (2004) is lower than the recommended benchmark of 2:1, but does represent an improvement upon the figure calculated for 2003. This could be a problem if it continues, since it indicates the inability of the company to meet its debts. It could be indicative of the nature of the company, since utility/service companies are unlikely to hold high levels of stocks, but rather incur high debtors levels or experience cash flow problems perhaps due to the nature of project/systems work. To properly evaluate this issue, we would need additional information regarding the make-up of elements of working capital. [3]

(v) **The gearing ratio: 252% (2003); 199% (2004)**

A value of 199% (2004) is high although it has fallen in comparison to 2003 (252%). It is higher than the recommended benchmark of 50%. This could be a problem if it continues, since it indicates the inability of the company to meet its debts. It could be indicative of the nature of the company, since utility/service companies are likely to hold high levels of debt or experience cash flow problems, perhaps due to the nature of project/systems work, or to invest in fixed asset base. To properly evaluate this ratio, we would need additional information regarding the make-up of debt. [3]

[15]

(c) The usefulness of ratio analysis can be evaluated with reference to the potential advantages of using financial ratios:

- The ratios give users of accounting statements an indication that there may be problems concerning liquidity and profitability.
- Quantitative measures facilitate assessment of the financial performance of the business across a range of areas.
- Comparisons can be made regarding financial performance over time.
- Comparisons can be made regarding financial performance relative to other businesses.
- Financial ratios can be used in addition to variance analysis to evaluate attainment of performance targets.

The usefulness of ratio analysis can be evaluated with reference to the potential drawbacks of using financial ratios:

- It may be difficult to make comparisons with similar businesses due to different accounting policies.
- Ratios are only as accurate as the underlying information in financial statements, and are thus subject to manipulation.
- Analysis is limited to quantitative issues, providing little information regarding rivals, etc.
- This ignores qualitative issues in the broader business environment and non-financial indicators, eg goodwill, reputation, quality, staff turnover.
- Alternative, reasonable arguments can also be accepted. [16]

Level 1 ([1]–[8])

Some knowledge and understanding of potential advantages and drawbacks of using financial ratios is demonstrated, with up to two points (any two points accepted) noted. Application of this knowledge to the question context is limited. Little or no evaluation evident. Quality of written communication is limited.

Level 2 ([9]–[12])

Adequate knowledge and understanding of potential advantages and drawbacks of using financial ratios is demonstrated, with up to three points noted (a balanced argument must be stated). There is some application of this knowledge to the question context and some evaluation evident. Quality of written communication is satisfactory.

Level 3 ([13]–[16])

Thorough knowledge and understanding of potential advantages and drawbacks of using financial ratios is demonstrated, with up to four points noted (a balanced argument must be stated). There is good application of this knowledge to the question context and evidence of points fully evaluated. Quality of written communication is of a high standard.

Maximum level 2 if no final judgement provided – typically stating that ratio analysis may/may not be of use in analysing final accounts. Maximum level 2 if no reference made to a company such as Viridian Group plc.

CHAPTER 4

Investment appraisal

One of the most important areas of long-term decision making that firms must tackle is investment. This is the decision to buy land, buildings, machinery, and so on in the hope of earning an income greater than the funds used to buy them. In order to make these decisions, firms must assess the outflows and inflows of the funds associated with the project, the life span of the investment, the risk associated with investing, and the cost of obtaining the funding to finance the project.

©iStockphoto.com/mikdam

When making a decision to invest, organisations will often carry out the following five steps:

1. Identify a project(s) to meet the firm's needs
2. Make an appraisal of the alternatives
3. Select the best alternative(s)
4. Invest in the chosen alternative(s)
5. Monitor the progress of the project(s)

Investment appraisal involves an organisation examining stage 3 and 4 of this process.

Investment appraisal methods

One of the most important steps of investment appraisal is to calculate if the benefits of investing large capital sums outweigh the costs of making the investment. There is a range of methods that a firm can use to help with this decision-making process. **Payback** and **net present value (NPV)** are two common methods of appraising the viability of an investment.

☐ PAYBACK

This method of investment appraisal calculates the amount of time it takes for the cash inflows from a capital investment project to equal the cash outflows. One way that a firm can decide between two or more competing projects is to choose the project that has the shortest **payback period**.

$$\text{payback period} = \frac{\text{initial payment}}{\text{annual cash inflow}}$$

For example, £10 million is invested in a project and it is forecasted that it will generate £500,000 per year.

The payback period is therefore:

$$\frac{£10,000,000}{£500,000} = 20 \text{ years}$$

Not all projects will generate even cash flows over their life spans. For example, a firm may be deciding whether or not to invest in a new piece of machinery costing £500,000, and the firm estimates that the machinery will generate income over the next five years as follows.

Year 1	Year 2	Year 3	Year 4	Year 5
£100,000	£125,000	£125,000	£150,000	£180,000

In this example the payback period is four years, ie:

£100,000 + £125,000 + £125,000 + £150,000 = £500,000

As stated earlier, if an organisation is faced with a range of possible projects it can use the payback method to choose the project with the shortest payback period.

For example, assume that an organisation is faced with three possible projects, all costing £140,000. The flow of income from these projects is as follows.

©iStockphoto.com/nyul

	Year 1	Year 2	Year 3	Year 4	Year 5	Year 6	Total
Project 1	£20,000	£20,000	£40,000	£40,000	£60,000	£80,000	£260,000
Project 2	£40,000	£40,000	£40,000	£40,000	£40,000	£40,000	£240,000
Project 3	£60,000	£60,000	£40,000	£20,000	£20,000	£20,000	£220,000

From this example, the organisation will choose project 3 because it has the shortest payback period, being slightly less than three years. Project 1's payback stretches into the fifth year, and project 2's into the fourth year.

It should be noted that this method does not take into account the total income from the projects, as project 3 has the lowest return over the six-year period.

There are both advantages and disadvantages of using the payback method of investment appraisal.

Advantages

- The method is useful for situations where technology changes rapidly, such as investment in new computers, and it is important to recover the cost of the investment as soon as possible.
- Payback is a simple method to use. Research over the years has shown that UK firms favour it and perhaps this is understandable given how easy it is to calculate.
- The method is useful to firms with cash flow problems as it allows them to pay back the investment more quickly than others.
- The method places more emphasis on early return forecasts which are likely to be more accurate than later forecasts.

Disadvantages

- Cash earned after the payback period is not taken into account.
- The method ignores the profitability of the project as the emphasis is placed on how quick the project is paid back.
- The method ignores the timing of the return prior to the payback.

Payback may be used as one of the first methods to assess competing projects. It can be used as an initial screening tool, but it is inappropriate as a basis for sophisticated investment decisions.

NET PRESENT VALUE (NPV)

The **NPV** method of investment appraisal takes into account the timing of returns as well as the size of the return from an investment.

For example, imagine your parents have offered you £250 if you are successful in your A2 Applied Business. If they give you the choice of accepting the money now or after you get your results, it is likely that you will take the money now.

There are many reasons for this:

- There may be some uncertainty as to whether you will pass your exams.
- The value of the money will be greater now than when your results come out.
- You could save the money and gain some interest on it.
- You could buy something now and get the benefit of it immediately, instead of having to wait until your results arrive.

These points form the basis of the concept known as the time concept of money. The £250 is worth more today than in the future or, if we look at this in another way, £250 in the future is worth less than it is today.

The NPV method of investment appraisal takes this into account. An investment will yield future streams of income, but a greater weighting is given to the returns in the early years than in later years.

The following formula may be used to calculate this weighting.

$$PV = \frac{A}{(1=r)\ n}$$

Where PV = present value
    r = the rate of discount
    n = the number of years
    A = the sum in question

Discount table

It is not essential to use the above formula to calculate the present value of future streams of income, as a discount table can be used to obtain the weighting (**discount factor**).

For example, a firm is considering investing in a piece of machinery costing £300,000 and it is assumed that a discount rate of 10% should be used. This project will result in net return of £100,000 per year over a five-year period. The machinery will be worthless after the five years.

Year	Cash flow (£000)	Discount factor	Present value (£000)
0	(300)	1	(300)
1	100	0.909	90.9
2	100	0.826	82.6
3	100	0.751	75.1
4	100	0.683	68.3
5	100	0.621	62.1
NPV			**79.0**

The discount factors are obtained from the discount table overleaf by reading off the year against the discount rate. For example, if a discount factor of 2% is used, £1 is worth 0.961 or 96.10 pence after two years.

In the table above, the discount factors were obtained assuming a 10% discount rate. The discount factors represent the present value of £1, so in order to find the present value of the future streams of income we multiply the incomes by the discount factors. In this case we are multiplying the discount factors by £100,000. This gives us the present values of the future five-year streams of £100,000.

The £300,000 represents the initial cost of the machinery. Its discount factor is 1 because it is being purchased now and so its value equals £300,000.

The NPV is obtained by adding up the present values of the future income streams and subtracting the initial cost from this. If the sum of the present values is greater than the initial cost, the NPV is positive. If this happens the project is worth investing in. If the NPV is negative, the project should not be undertaken.

If there is a choice of projects, the one with the highest positive NPV should be chosen.

There are both advantages and disadvantages of using the NPV method of investment appraisal.

Advantages

- NPV uses the time concept of money.
- The entire life of the project is taken into account.
- The method allows comparisons to be made with other opportunities.

Disadvantages

- The calculations are complex.
- It may be difficult to decide upon the most appropriate discount factor to use.
- Managers may have difficulty in understanding the technique.

OTHER CONSIDERATIONS

The techniques discussed in this chapter assume that the organisation is going to purchase the new asset. This may not always be the case as leasing may be an option for the organisation. There are, however, both advantages and disadvantages associated with leasing. These were discussed on page 6.

Year	Rate (%)													
	1	2	3	4	5	6	7	8	9	10	12	14	15	20
1	0.990	0.980	0.971	0.962	0.952	0.943	0.935	0.926	0.917	0.909	0.893	0.877	0.870	0.833
2	0.980	0.961	0.943	0.925	0.907	0.890	0.873	0.857	0.842	0.826	0.797	0.769	0.756	0.694
3	0.971	0.942	0.915	0.889	0.864	0.840	0.816	0.794	0.772	0.751	0.712	0.675	0.658	0.579
4	0.961	0.924	0.888	0.855	0.823	0.792	0.763	0.735	0.708	0.683	0.636	0.592	0.572	0.482
5	0.951	0.906	0.863	0.822	0.784	0.747	0.713	0.681	0.650	0.621	0.567	0.519	0.497	0.402
6	0.942	0.888	0.837	0.790	0.746	0.705	0.666	0.630	0.596	0.564	0.507	0.456	0.432	0.335
7	0.933	0.871	0.813	0.760	0.711	0.665	0.623	0.583	0.547	0.513	0.452	0.400	0.376	0.279
8	0.923	0.853	0.789	0.731	0.677	0.627	0.582	0.540	0.502	0.467	0.404	0.351	0.327	0.233
9	0.914	0.837	0.766	0.703	0.645	0.592	0.544	0.500	0.460	0.424	0.361	0.308	0.284	0.194
10	0.905	0.820	0.744	0.676	0.614	0.558	0.508	0.463	0.422	0.386	0.322	0.270	0.247	0.162
11	0.896	0.804	0.722	0.650	0.585	0.527	0.475	0.429	0.388	0.350	0.287	0.237	0.215	0.135
12	0.887	0.788	0.701	0.625	0.557	0.497	0.444	0.397	0.356	0.319	0.257	0.208	0.187	0.112
13	0.879	0.773	0.681	0.601	0.530	0.469	0.415	0.368	0.326	0.290	0.229	0.182	0.163	0.093
14	0.870	0.758	0.661	0.577	0.505	0.442	0.388	0.340	0.299	0.263	0.205	0.160	0.141	0.078
15	0.861	0.743	0.642	0.555	0.481	0.417	0.362	0.315	0.275	0.239	0.183	0.140	0.123	0.065
16	0.853	0.728	0.623	0.534	0.458	0.394	0.339	0.292	0.252	0.218	0.163	0.123	0.107	0.054
17	0.844	0.714	0.605	0.513	0.436	0.371	0.317	0.270	0.231	0.198	0.146	0.108	0.093	0.045
18	0.836	0.700	0.587	0.494	0.416	0.350	0.296	0.250	0.212	0.180	0.130	0.095	0.081	0.038
19	0.828	0.686	0.570	0.475	0.396	0.331	0.277	0.232	0.194	0.164	0.116	0.083	0.070	0.031
20	0.820	0.673	0.554	0.456	0.377	0.312	0.258	0.215	0.178	0.149	0.104	0.073	0.061	0.026

ACTIVITY 4.1

Investment appraisal

The boost in sales for Starlight Ltd's range of dark chocolates had been unexpected. The report linking dark chocolate with chemicals that protect the heart seemed to have had an unexpected benefit and turned many consumers towards the natural organic chocolate produced by the firm.

Market research suggested that this was not going to be a short-term fad and forecasts of future sales were healthy. The board had decided to accept the recommendation of the sales and production team and invest in a new piece of equipment for the production line that would automate some of the work currently carried out by staff on the line. Those staff could be better utilised elsewhere in the plant and, in addition, it would speed up the production and help meet the expected demand.

The investigations into the supplier of such a piece of equipment had identified four possible sources:

Machine 1:
A German firm producing a high precision piece of equipment with software allowing different production runs to be catered for

Machine 2:
The same equipment without the software option secured from a firm in Taiwan

Machine 3:
A different machine manufactured in Armenia – significantly cheaper!

Machine 4:
Another machine with a different specification but which is suitable for the job required, produced by a firm in the US

The costs associated with each machine are as follows.

Dark chocolate shown to boost heart-protecting antioxidants in the blood

©iStockphoto.com/Leah-Anne Thompson

	Machine 1 £	Machine 2 £	Machine 3 £	Machine 4 £
Initial cost	550,000	550,000	290,000	460,000
Expected cash flow				
Year 1	20,000	50,000	15,000	30,000
Year 2	75,000	175,000	80,000	95,000
Year 3	125,000	200,000	120,000	150,000
Year 4	250,000	175,000	100,000	210,000
Year 5	200,000	70,000	60,000	300,000

The firm believes that the likely discount rate will be 5%. The discount tables for selected rates are shown in the table overleaf.

Year	Rate (%)			
	4.5	5.0	5.5	6.0
1	0.9569378	0.9523810	0.9478673	0.9433962
2	0.9157300	0.9070295	0.8984524	0.8899964
3	0.8762966	0.8638376	0.8516137	0.8396193
4	0.8385613	0.8227025	0.8072167	0.7920937
5	0.8024510	0.7835262	0.7651344	0.7472582

The task:

Your task is to present an argued case for one of the machines that the firm should invest in.

You should use at least two appropriate methods of investment appraisal in your presentation and you should highlight the relative costs and benefits of each method.

Advise the board on other factors that will need to be considered in taking the decision in addition to the quantitative analysis given above.

(Activity adapted from www.bized.co.uk)

PAST PAPER QUESTIONS

1. Study the information below and answer the questions that follow.

Anne works as a finance manager for Belfast Bakeries. The business wishes to invest in a new machine to produce apple pies. Pete, the production manager, meets Anne to review the estimated production, sales and costing data. He has obtained the following information related to this investment project:

	Year 1	Year 2	Year 3
No. of apple pies produced/sold	100,000	100,000	50,000
Sales revenues	£35,000	£45,000	£22,500
Variable costs	£5,000	£15,000	£7,500

The cost of the new machine is £600,000, paid at the start of the project. The new machine is expected to depreciate by £20,000 per year for each year of the project. The discount factor to be used is 10%. The relevant discount factors are summarised as follows.

Year	10% DF
1	0.9091
2	0.8264
3	0.7513

It may be assumed that all cash flows occur evenly throughout each year and that normal conventions apply regarding the use of discounting.

Unfortunately, Anne has taken ill during the meeting, and has asked you, as her deputy, to assist Pete in reviewing the project. Anne had already started work on the detailed calculations, and you are required to finish her workings as far as the information permits.

Note: candidates may present their calculations/workings rounded to the nearest '£' throughout subsections (a), (b) and (c) as appropriate.

(a) Calculate the (undiscounted) payback period for this project:

	Annual net cash flow (£)	Cumulative net cash flow (£)
Initial investment	(60,000)	(60,000)
Year 1	30,000	(30,000)
Year 2		
Year 3		15,000

Payback period is: _____ [4]

(b) Calculate the accounting rate of return (ARR) for this project:

Total sales revenues (£)	[ ]
Less: total variable costs (£)	[ ]
Less: total depreciation (£)	60,000
Total profit	[ ]
Initial investment	60,000
Accounting rate of return (%)	[ ] [4]

Note: Accounting Rate of Return may be calculated as ...

(total profit/initial investment) × 100%.

(c) Calculate the net present value (NPV) of this project:

Year	Annual net cash flow (£)	Discount factor (10%)	Present value (£)
1	30,000	0.9091	[ ]
2	[ ]	0.8264	[ ]
3	[ ]	0.7513	[ ]
		Total present value	[ ]
		Less: initial investment	60,000
		Net present value	[ ] [7]

(d) With reference to your calculations and other related issues, evaluate the investment as proposed, stating clearly your final recommendation to Pete. [12]

PAST PAPER ANSWERS

1. Note: candidates have been instructed to present answers rounded to the nearest '£' for ease of calculation/working. Answers which have not been rounded may be accepted provided they are reasonably accurate (+/–£5.00).

(a)

	Annual net cash flow (£)	Cumulative net cash flow (£)	
Initial investment	(60,000)	(60,000)	
Year 1	30,000	(30,000)	
Year 2	**30,000**	**0**	[2]
Year 3	**15,000**	15,000	[1]

Payback period is: 2 years [1]

([1] for each figure stated; [1] for correctly calculating payback period; 4×[1]) [4]

(b)

Total sales revenues (£)	**102,500**	[1]
Less: total variable costs (£)	**27,500**	[1]
Less: total depreciation (£)	60,000	
Total profit	**15,000**	[1]
Initial investment	60,000	
Accounting rate of return (%)	**25%**	[1]

([1] for each figure stated; [1] for correctly calculating ARR; 4×[1]) [4]

(c)

Year	Annual net cash flow (£)	Discount factor (10%)	Present value (£)	
1	30,000	0.9091	**27,273.00**	[1]
2	**30,000**	0.8264	**24,792.00**	[2]
3	**15,000**	0.7513	**11,269.50**	[2]
		Total present value	63,334.5	[1]
		Less: initial investment	(60,000)	
		Net present value (NPV)	**3,334.50**	[1]

([1] for each figure stated; [1] for correctly calculating NPV; 7×[1]) [7]

(d)
- Recommend: the project acceptable and should proceed.
- Project payback is within two years.
- Project ARR is 25%.
- Project NPV is £3,334.50 which is positive.
- The project appears to be acceptable irrespective of which investment appraisal method is adopted.
- The most reliable method is NPV/discounting, as it adjusts for risk, and various other factors, eg time value of money.
- Issues include accuracy of cash flow forecasts, sales revenues, costs and project timescales.
- The machine appears to depreciate rapidly over the life span.
- Other reasonable/relevant points are also acceptable. [12]

Level 1: ([1]–[3])

Some knowledge and understanding of the alternative methods of investment appraisal and some application to case. One issue properly explained. There is little attempt to analyse or evaluate the advantages. Quality of written communication is limited.

Level 2: ([4]–[6])

Adequate knowledge and understanding of the alternative methods of investment appraisal is demonstrated and there is a reasonable attempt to apply to case study. Up to two issues are properly explained. Some attempt is made to analyse or evaluate the advantages. Quality of written communication is satisfactory.

Level 3: ([7]–[12])

Good knowledge and understanding of the alternative methods of investment appraisal is demonstrated and there is appropriate application in the context of the case. Three or more issues are properly explained within the context of the case. The issues are thoroughly analysed and there is a comprehensive and perceptive evaluation of their relative merits, including final judgement. Quality of written communication is of a high standard.

Maximum Level 2 if no application to the unique situation of the case.

PAST PAPER QUESTIONS

2. Dave is a financial analyst advising Antrim Coast Bus Tours Ltd on the purchase of a new bus. He supplies you with the following data (Table 1) relating to two options under consideration:

Table 1: Financial data

Panel A:	Bus 1	Bus 2
Initial investment	£50,000	£50,000
Cash flows:		
Year 1	35,000	20,000
Year 2	30,000	20,000
Year 3	25,000	24,000
Year 4	30,000	46,000
Panel B:		
Discount factors (10%)		
Year 1	0.909	0.909
Year 2	0.826	0.826
Year 3	0.751	0.751
Year 4	0.683	0.683

(a) Dave had started to calculate the net present value (NPV) for each bus when he had to take a leave of absence to attend a training course, leaving some of the initial calculations unfinished. In the meantime, Matt (the managing director) was planning the next month's bus tours and wanted to know which bus to purchase.

In order to assist Matt, you are required to complete the following tables which Dave had started.

(i) Bus 1: NPV calculations

Year	Cash inflows (£)	Discount factor (10%)	Present value (£)
1	35,000	0.909	
2	30,000	0.826	
3	25,000	0.751	
4	30,000	0.683	
Initial investment			(50,000)
Net present value (£)			

[5]

(ii) Bus 2: NPV calculations

Year	Cash inflows (£)	Discount factor (10%)	Present value (£)
1	20,000	0.909	
2	20,000	0.826	
3		0.751	
4		0.683	
		Initial investment	(50,000)
		Net present value (£)	

[7]

(b) Matt had requested that the payback period be calculated in addition to the NPV, in order to assist his decision making.

Using the data presented in Table 1, you are required to calculate the payback period for each bus.

(i) Bus 1: payback period   [2]

(ii) Bus 2: payback period   [2]

(c) Advise Matt which proposal you think is best in financial terms.   [3]

(d) Evaluate the following two methods of investment appraisal used by Antrim Coast Bus Tours Ltd.

(i) Payback period   [7]

(ii) Net present value   [7]

PAST PAPER ANSWERS

2. (a) (i) Bus 1: NPV calculations

Year	Cash inflows (£)	Discount factor (10%)	Present value (£)
1	35,000	0.909	**31,815**
2	30,000	0.826	**24,780**
3	25,000	0.751	**18,775**
4	30,000	0.683	**20,490**
		Initial investment	(50,000)
		Net present value (£)	**45,860**

[5]

(ii) Bus 2: NPV calculations

Year	Cash inflows (£)	Discount factor (10%)	Present value (£)
1	20,000	0.909	**18,180**
2	20,000	0.826	**16,520**
3	**24,000**	0.751	**18,024**
4	**46,000**	0.683	**31,418**
		Initial investment	(50,000)
		Net present value (£)	**34,142**

[7]

(b) (i) Bus 1: payback period:

1.5 years

(1 + (15,000/30,000)) [2]

(ii) Bus 2: payback period:

2.4 years

(2 + (10,000/24,000))

Acceptable range of answers: 2.4–2.6 years [2]; figures rounded to 3 years [1] [2]

(c) Bus 1 is the best project, and is the bus which should be purchased, since it yields the highest NPV and the shortest payback period.

([1] for correct conclusion; [2] for suitable explanation of decision arrived at) [3]

(d) (i) Payback period:

- Relatively simple to understand
- Reasonably straightforward to calculate
- Most managers familiar with concept of cash flows
- Alternative arguments are also acceptable [7]

Level 1: ([1]–[2])

Some knowledge and understanding of merits of alternative investment appraisal methods noted is demonstrated but this is limited. Application of this knowledge to the question context, if present, is very limited. Quality of written communication is limited. (One to two points accepted.)

Level 2: ([3]–[5])

Adequate knowledge and understanding of merits of alternative investment appraisal methods noted is demonstrated. There is some application of this knowledge to the question context. Quality of written communication is satisfactory. (Two to three points accepted.)

Level 3: ([6]–[7])

Thorough knowledge and understanding of merits of alternative investment appraisal methods noted is demonstrated. There is good application of knowledge to the question context. Quality of written communication is of a high standard. (Three plus points accepted.)

(ii) Net present value:

- Considers the time value of money
- Adjusts for risk
- Utilises concept of cash flows, yielding maximum value for company
- Alternative arguments are also acceptable [7]

(Levels as above)

CHAPTER 5

Absorption costing

When a business is involved in production, it will incur many different costs. These costs can be either internal or external. External costs arise when a business needs to pay for raw materials that have been bought from outside the business. Internal costs arise when a service is bought from another department within the organisation.

All of these costs must be recorded where they occur and these are known as **cost centres**.

There are different ways that cost centres can be classified:

- As a geographical location such as a factory, a sales region, or a department
- As a person such as a director, a salesperson or a maintenance worker
- As an item of equipment such as a photocopier, telephone line or a vehicle

Costs may be direct or indirect:

- **Direct costs** – these costs are amounts of expenditure that can be identified with a specific product or project. Examples of direct costs are raw materials, packaging and direct labour.

- **Indirect costs** – these costs cannot be identified directly with a particular product or project. They are associated with the whole business and can be referred to as overheads, for example rent, insurance, salaries of office staff, and rates.

©iStockphoto.com/vicnt

Absorption costing attempts to identify all of the costs associated with an activity. The charging of direct costs is very simple, as it is easy to identify the exact value of the cost and align it with the activity in question. However, the charging of indirect costs is more complicated. One method of allocating indirect costs involves absorption costing.

Absorption costing involves charging or 'absorbing' all of the relative indirect costs associated with a business activity and adding these to the activity's direct costs. There is a range of ways of apportioning these costs and the chosen method will depend upon the nature of the cost in question:

- Costs such as rent, rates, heating and lighting can be apportioned according to the area or volume in a building that the operation occupies.
- Personnel expenses may be apportioned according to the number of people involved in the operation.
- Depreciation and insurance costs could be apportioned according to the book value of the assets in question.

Summary of common methods of apportionment

Overhead	Basis of apportionment
Rent, rates	Area taken up by the activity
Heating costs	Volume occupied
Cost of personnel administration	Number of employees involved
Indirect labour used	In proportion to direct labour
Insurance, depreciation	In proportion to the value of capital

Job costing

The full cost of a particular job is the sum of direct costs and the share of the indirect costs associated with the job.

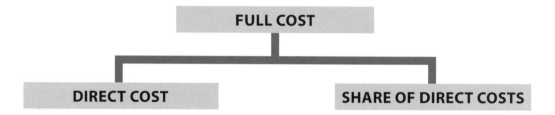

Job costing is therefore the process of calculating the full cost of a job by identifying the direct cost of the job and adding this to the share of indirect costs.

This is illustrated by the example below:

- Zeemobile Ltd manufactures mobile phones.
- The business has overheads of £10,000 each month.
- Each month 1,000 direct labour hours are worked.
- Each phone manufactured by the business uses direct materials costing £15.
- A telephone takes 3 hours to manufacture and the direct labour associated with this is £8 per hour.
- Overheads are charged on a direct labour hour basis.

©iStockphoto.com/hidesy

What is the cost of manufacturing each phone?

Solution

The overhead absorption rate (OAR) is £10. This is because overheads are £10,000 each month and 1,000 direct labour hours are worked each month (10,000/1,000).

Each telephone takes 3 hours to produce.

	£
Direct materials	15
Direct labour (3 hours × £8)	24
Total direct costs	39
Overheads (3 hours × £10)	30
Full cost of job	**69**

The full cost of the job is calculated by adding the two direct costs (materials and labour) to the proportion of indirect costs (overheads).

METHOD OF APPORTIONING INDIRECT COSTS

On the basis of selling price

Marketing costs are often apportioned on this basis because their aim is to increase sales.

To apportion according to sales the following formula may be used.

$$\frac{\text{cost of operation to be apportioned}}{\text{total sales}} \times \text{sales of each operation}$$

For example, a hotel has the following sales for a month.

	£
Rooms	50,000
Restaurant	20,000
Bar	5,000
Total	**75,000**

The total marketing costs are £6,000.

Solution

$$\text{Rooms} = \frac{6,000}{75,000} \times 50,000 = 4,000$$

$$\text{Restaurant} = \frac{6,000}{75,000} \times 20,000 = 1,600$$

$$\text{Bars} = \frac{6,000}{75,000} \times 5,000 = 400$$

$$\textbf{Total} = \textbf{6,000}$$

The Merchant Hotel, Belfast

On the basis of floor area

This method is suitable for expenses which change according to the physical size of the department. Examples would include heating and lighting, and insurance.

To apportion according to floor area, the following formula may be used.

$$\frac{\text{cost of operation to be apportioned}}{\text{total floor areas}} \times \text{sales of each operation}$$

For example, a college has the following floor areas.

	m²
Classrooms	4,000
Canteen	1,000
Library	1,000
Leisure facilities	2,000
Total floor area	**8,000**

The heating and lighting bill for one month is £5,000.

Solution

$$\text{Classrooms} = \frac{5,000}{8,000} \times 4,000 = £2,500$$

$$\text{Canteen} = \frac{5,000}{8,000} \times 1,000 = £625$$

$$\text{Library} = \frac{5,000}{8,000} \times 1,000 = £625$$

$$\text{Leisure facilities} = \frac{5,000}{8,000} \times 2,000 = £1,250$$

$$\textbf{Total} = \textbf{£5,000}$$

©iStockphoto.com/vasiliki

On the basis of direct labour costs

This method is suitable for apportioning indirect labour or costs connected with labour such as personnel and training costs.

To apportion according to direct labour costs, the following formula may be used.

$$\frac{\text{cost of operation to be apportioned}}{\text{total direct labour costs}} \times \text{direct labour cost of each operation}$$

For example, the direct labour costs for a hotel are as follows.

	£
Rooms	15,000
Restaurant	12,000
Bars	4,000
Leisure facilities	2,500
Total labour costs	**33,500**

The **total cost** of training the entire staff is £2,520.

Solution

$$\text{Rooms} = \frac{2,520}{33,500} \times 15,000 = £1,128.36$$

$$\text{Restaurant} = \frac{2,520}{33,500} \times 12,000 = £902.69$$

$$\text{Bars} = \frac{2,520}{33,500} \times 4,000 = £300.90$$

$$\text{Leisure facilities} = \frac{2,520}{33,500} \times 2,500 = £188.06$$

Total $= £2,520.01$

©iStockphoto.com/terex

On the basis of direct labour hours

This method is suitable for apportioning indirect costs associated with manufacturing items.

For example, Hotflow Ltd is a small manufacturing firm that produces boilers for central heating systems. The organisation has estimated that the following costs are going to be incurred during the next month.

Indirect labour costs	£9,000
Direct labour time	6,000 hours
Depreciation of machinery	£3,000
Rent and rates	£5,000
Direct labour costs	£30,000
Heating and lighting	£2,000
Machine time	2,000 hours
Indirect materials	£500
Miscellaneous costs	£200
Direct materials costs	£3,000

Each boiler that is produced takes 12 direct labour hours and uses 20 kilograms of lead costing £2 per kilogram.

Using direct labour hours as a basis of charging overheads, what is the full cost of making each boiler?

©iStockphoto.com/inhauscreative

Solution

The first step involves identifying the indirect costs and totalling them.

	£
Indirect labour costs	9,000
Depreciation of machinery	3,000
Rent and rates	5,000
Heating and lighting	2,000
Indirect materials	500
Miscellaneous costs	200
Total indirect cost	**19,700**

The total direct labour time is 6,000 hours.

Using the direct labour hour basis of charging overheads to jobs, the indirect cost recovery rate per labour hour is as follows.

$$\frac{\textbf{total indirect costs}}{\textbf{total direct labour time}} \longrightarrow \frac{£19,700}{6,000} = £3.28 \text{ per direct labour hour}$$

The full cost of each boiler is as follows.

	£
Direct materials (20 × £2)	40.00
Direct labour (12 × (£30,000/6,000))	60.00
Indirect costs (12 × £3.28)	39.36
Total cost	**139.36**

On the basis of machine hours

This method may also be suitable for apportioning indirect costs associated with manufacturing items.

For example, if Hotflow Ltd used machine hours as a basis of charging overheads, what is the full cost of making each boiler?

Solution

As when using direct labour hours to apportion indirect costs, the first step involves identifying the indirect costs and totalling them (see above). The total indirect costs are the same, irrespective of which method of apportionment is used.

Using the machine hour basis of charging overheads to jobs, the overhead recovery rate on a machine hour basis is as follows.

$$\frac{\textbf{total indirect costs}}{\textbf{total machine hours}} \longrightarrow \frac{£19,700}{2,000} = £9.85 \text{ per machine hour}$$

The full cost of each boiler is as follows.

	£
Direct materials (20 × £2)	40.00
Direct labour (12 × (£30,000/6,000))	60.00
Indirect costs (12 × £9.85)	118.20
Total cost	**218.20**

Although the absorption method of costing is a popular method of costing, there are some criticisms of its use. When a firm produces a wide range of products it may make the apportionment of direct costs difficult. Any method of apportionment will also be arbitrary so it is important for a business to be consistent in the way that it apportions its indirect costs.

REVISION QUESTION

Mugs Ltd's overhead costs are shown below.

	£
Heating and lighting	6,000
Building insurance	1,500
Depreciation of assets	10,000
Building repairs	4,500
Rent and rates	6,600
Wages	52,020

The company has two departments – production and finishing. The following information is also available.

Department	Production	Finishing
Floor space (m²)	40	20
Book value of assets (£)	60,000	40,000
Number of employees	15	10

(a) Copy and complete the table below to show how the overheads will be apportioned between the production and finishing departments.

Overhead	Basis of apportionment	Total	Production	Finishing
Heating and lighting				
Building insurance				
Depreciation of assets				
Building repairs				
Rent and rates				
Wages				
Total				

(b) If the estimated output was 80,000 units, how much of the cost would be absorbed by the production department and by the finishing department per unit?

PAST PAPER QUESTIONS

1. Study the information below and answer the questions that follow.

Chatterbox Ltd produces and sells mobile phones from a production plant located in Cushendall. The plant is divided into two operations – production and assembly. Each mobile handset requires two hours of production time and one hour of assembly time. The direct labour costs in the production department are £4 per hour, while direct labour costs in the assembly department are £5 per hour.

However, a problem with the computer software has meant that neither the reallocation of the stores department's overheads (Table 1) nor the overhead absorption rates (Table 2) can be calculated.

The following financial information (Table 1) related to the production of mobile phones has been summarised and relevant total expenditures calculated, using the company's new financial information system.

It is known that the total number of 'store issue notes' issued to the production department were 10,000, while the number issued to the assembly department were 5,000. Management has agreed that this will be the basis upon which to allocate the stores department's costs to other departments.

In addition, the total direct labour hours worked within the company were 100,000, subdivided between the production department (60,000) and the assembly department (40,000).

(a) You are required to complete Table 1 to show the production overhead analysis and apportionment of overheads for Chatterbox Ltd.

Table 1: Chatterbox Ltd production overheads analysis and apportionment

Overhead	Bases of apportionment	Total cost (£)	Production dept (£)	Assembly dept (£)	Stores dept (£)
Indirect wages	Direct	80,000	36,000	24,000	20,000
Indirect material	Direct	92,000	60,000	31,000	1,000
Catering costs	Direct	56,000	30,000	16,000	10,000
Rent and rates	Area	56,000	22,400	11,200	22,400
Depreciation	Plant cost	60,000	30,000	24,000	6,000
Power	Power use	50,000	35,000	7,500	7,500
Heat and light	Area	6,000	2,400	1,200	2,400
Health and safety costs	Number of staff	60,000	30,000	18,000	12,000
		460,000	245,800	132,900	81,300
Store	Store issue notes	0			
Total overheads					

[6]

(b) You are required to complete Table 2, to show the appropriate rates of overhead recovery for:

(i) The production department

(ii) The assembly department

Table 2: Overhead absorption rates

	Production dept	Assembly dept
Direct labour hours		
Total overheads (£)		
Overhead rate per direct labour hour (£)		

[6]

(c) You are required to comment briefly on the suitability of using:
   (i) A labour hour rate [4]
   (ii) A machine hour rate [4]

PAST PAPER ANSWERS

1. (a)   Table 1: Chatterbox Ltd production overheads analysis and apportionment

Overhead	Bases of apportionment	Total cost (£)	Production dept (£)	Assembly dept (£)	Stores dept (£)
Indirect wages	Direct	80,000	36,000	24,000	20,000
Indirect material	Direct	92,000	60,000	31,000	1,000
Catering costs	Direct	56,000	30,000	16,000	10,000
Rent and rates	Area	56,000	22,400	11,200	22,400
Depreciation	Plant cost	60,000	30,000	24,000	6,000
Power	Power use	50,000	35,000	7,500	7,500
Heat and light	Area	6,000	2,400	1,200	2,400
Health and safety costs	Number of staff	60,000	30,000	18,000	12,000
		460,000	245,800	132,900	81,300
Store	Store issue notes	0	**54,200**	**27,100**	**−81,300**
Total overheads		**460,000**	**300,000**	**160,000**	

[6]

[1] for each item correctly stated/calculated:

• Production dept apportionment of stores overheads (£54,200)
• Assembly dept apportionment of stores overheads (£27,100)
• Stores dept total overheads to be apportioned (£81,300)
• Total overheads (£460,000)
• Total production dept overheads (£300,000)
• Total assembly dept overheads (£160,000)

(b)   Table 2: Overhead absorption rates

	Production dept	Assembly dept
Direct labour hours	60,000	40,000
Total overheads (£)	300,000	160,000
Overhead rate per direct labour hour (£)	5	4

[1] for each item correctly stated/calculated:

- Production dept direct labour hours (60,000)
- Assembly dept direct labour hours (40,000)
- Total production dept overheads (£300,000)
- Total assembly dept overheads (£160,000)
- Overhead absorption rate for production dept (£5)
- Overhead absorption rate for assembly dept (£4)   [6]

(c) (i) Labour hour rate:

A labour hour rate is related to the amount of time jobs spend in each department and is appropriate when labour hours of the department are the predominant activity and the majority of overheads are related to labour activity. If these circumstances do not apply, then the direct machine overhead hour rate is recommended.   [4]

(ii) Machine hour rate:

A machine hour rate is related to the amount of time jobs spend in each department and is appropriate when machine hours of the department are the predominant activity and the majority of overheads are related to machinery. If these circumstances do not apply, then the direct labour overhead hour rate is recommended.   [4]

[8]

Level 1: ([1]–[3])

Some knowledge and understanding of concept of hourly rates is demonstrated, whether on machine or labour hour basis. There is little or no attempt to explain how they differ, or apply within context of case examined.

Level 2: ([4]–[6])

Adequate knowledge and understanding of concept of hourly rates is demonstrated, whether on machine or labour hour basis, and there is a reasonable attempt to explain how they differ. There is some application to the context of the case examined. Quality of written communication is satisfactory.

Level 3: ([7]–[8])

A thorough knowledge and understanding of concept of hourly rates is demonstrated, whether on machine or labour hour basis. There is clear awareness of how they differ. There is appropriate application to the context of the case examined. Quality of written communication is of a high standard.

PAST PAPER QUESTIONS

2. Wendy is a manager in a local company called V-Games Ltd which produces and sells the GoPad, a video games console aimed at a wide range of consumers. The console is in competition with widely-known brands such as the Sony Playstation®, the Nintendo GameCube, and the Xbox. Wendy is in the process of reviewing production costs of the GoPad and has provided you with the following costing data, summarised in Table 1:

Table 1: GoPad cost data

Direct material	£1,000,000
Direct labour	£2,000,000
Total production overheads	£2,000,000
Direct labour hours	500,000
Direct machine hours	400,000

In addition, Wendy supplies you with some data related to batch 999, which she selected at random for audit purposes. This is summarised in Table 2:

Table 2: Batch 999 GoPad cost data

Direct material	£60,000
Direct labour	£30,000
Total production overheads	–
Direct labour hours	7,500
Direct machine hours	7,500

(a) Using the information presented in Table 1, you are required to calculate the direct material overhead rate (percentage) based on the following formula:

$$\frac{\text{total production overheads}}{\text{total material costs}} \times 100\% \qquad \frac{\boxed{}}{\boxed{}} \times 100\%$$

Direct material overhead rate: _____ %   [3]

(b) Using the information presented in Table 1, you are required to calculate the machine hour overhead rate based on the following formula:

$$\frac{\text{total production overheads}}{\text{total machine hours}} \qquad \frac{\boxed{}}{\boxed{}}$$

Machine hour overhead rate: £ _____   [3]

(c) Using the information presented in Table 2, you are required to calculate the overheads which should be charged to production batch 999, using the direct material overhead rate (percentage):

materials charged to batch 999 × direct material overhead rate

☐	× ☐

Overhead cost charged to batch 999: £ _____ [3]

(d) Using the information presented in Table 2, you are required to calculate the overheads which should be charged to production batch 999, using the machine hour overhead rate:

machine hours used in batch 999 × machine hour overhead rate

☐	× ☐

Overhead cost charged to batch 999: £ _____ [3]

(e) Discuss the extent to which the following methods of overhead absorption are suitable for use by V-Games Ltd.
   (i) Direct material overhead rate [4]
   (ii) Machine hour overhead rate [4]

PAST PAPER ANSWERS

2. (a)
$$\frac{£2,000,000}{£1,000,000} \times 100\%$$

Direct material overhead rate: **200%**

([1] for each figure stated; 3×[1]) [3]

(b)
$$\frac{£2,000,000}{400,000}$$

Machine hour overhead rate: **£5.00**

([1] for each figure stated; 3×[1]) [3]

(c) **£60,000 × 200%**

Overhead cost charged to batch 999: **£120,000**

([1] for each figure stated; 3×[1]) [3]

(d) **7,500 × £5.00**

Overhead cost charged to batch 999: **£37,500**

([1] for each figure stated; 3×[1]) [3]

(e) (i) Direct material overhead rate:

- Overhead recovery should normally relate to the amount of time jobs spend in various departments, thus the percentage direct material method cannot be recommended.
- For example, batch 999 requires £60,000 of material, using 7,500 machine hours; thus a job requiring £10,000 of material using 15,000 hours (twice the hours of batch 999) would be charged £20,000 for overheads (one sixth of the amount charged to batch 999). [4]

Level 1: ([1])

Some knowledge and understanding of use of alternative overhead absorption rates is demonstrated but this is limited. Application of this knowledge to the question context, if present, is very limited. Quality of written communication is limited.

Level 2: ([3])

Adequate knowledge and understanding of use of alternative overhead absorption rates is demonstrated. There is some application of this knowledge to the question context. Quality of written communication is satisfactory.

Level 3: ([4])

Thorough knowledge and understanding of use of alternative overhead absorption rates is demonstrated. There is good application of knowledge to the question context. Quality of written communication is of a high standard.

(ii) Machine hour overhead rate:

- Machine hour rate is related to the amount of time jobs spend in each department and is appropriate when machine hours of the department are the predominant activity and the majority of overhead expenses are related to machinery.
- If these circumstances do not apply, then the direct labour overhead hour rate is recommended. [4]

(Levels as above)

CHAPTER 6

Breakeven analysis

The **breakeven** is the point at which a firm makes neither a profit nor a loss. This type of analysis is important for a firm as it will indicate how many units of a product or service are needed for the firm to break even.

Before the breakeven can be calculated, it is necessary to understand the difference between **fixed costs** and **variable costs**.

Fixed costs

These are costs that remain the same irrespective of output levels, for example rent, rates, and salaries. Graphically, they are represented by a horizontal line, reinforcing the fact that the costs do not change as output changes.

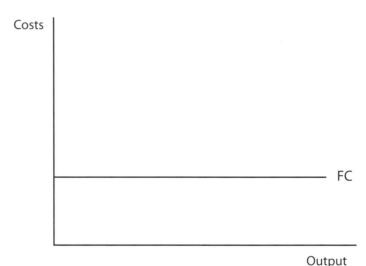

Variable costs

These are costs that change as output levels change, for example raw materials, direct labour, and electricity. Graphically, they are represented by a diagonal line that cuts the origin, showing the costs increasing as output levels rise.

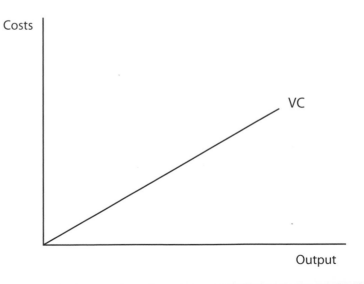

Semi-variable costs

Some costs cannot readily be classified as fixed or variable and are classified as **semi-variable** costs. An example of a semi-variable cost would be a telephone bill which is made up of two different types of charges. Part of the bill is for line rental which is fixed for the period in question. The other part of the bill is the charge for the given number of calls that have been made. Therefore, the telephone bill has an element of fixed cost and an element of variable cost associated with it.

Total costs

The **total costs** are calculated by adding the fixed costs and the variable costs. Again, these are represented by a diagonal line, except the line cuts the y-axis at the same point as the fixed cost line. This is because fixed costs will still need to be paid even at the point where there is no output.

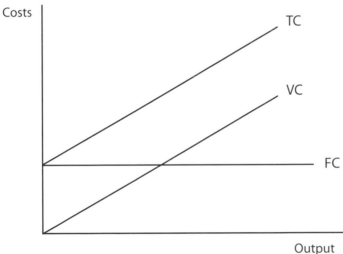

Calculating the breakeven

It is vital for a business to know what output level or sales level is necessary before it breaks even. However, breakeven analysis does not specify the time that it will take to reach this level. This will depend on how quickly sales are generated and in some cases it can be many years before a firm will reach its breakeven sales level.

In order to work out the breakeven, it is essential to know various pieces of information:

- The price being charged
- The variable costs
- The fixed costs

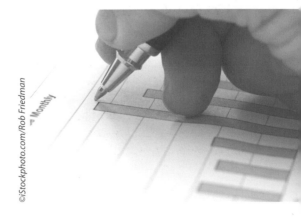

Consider the example in the table below.

	£
Price	5
Variable costs (per unit)	3
Fixed costs	2,000

This information tells us that every time one unit is sold there is an excess of income over variable costs of £2. This figure is called the **contribution**.

contribution = selling price per unit – variable cost per unit

However, this is *not* the same as profit, because the fixed costs of £2,000 also have to be paid. It is therefore necessary to work out how many units need to be sold for the total contribution to be equal to the fixed costs.

In this case, the contribution is £2 per unit and the fixed costs are £2,000, so if we can sell 1,000 units we will have enough contribution to pay the fixed costs. Any units we sell beyond that level will then make a profit of £2 each. So if we sell 1,001 units our total profit will be £2, if we sell 1,002 units our total profit will be £4, and so on.

The **breakeven** level of output can therefore be calculated from the following formula.

$$\text{breakeven output} = \frac{\text{fixed costs}}{\text{contribution (per unit)}}$$

The breakeven level of output can also be obtained by plotting the figures on a graph. This is done by following the steps below.

Stage 1

Plot the **total cost** line. Remember that this will be the sum of the fixed costs and variable costs. This means that it will start from part way up the y-axis (at the fixed costs point).

Stage 2

Add the total revenue curve. This can be plotted by working out the total revenue at the maximum capacity of the firm, for example if it can produce 50,000 units of a good and sells them at £28 each, then the TR line will go from the origin to a point given by 50,000 units and £1.4 million.

The graph should now look like the example on the right.

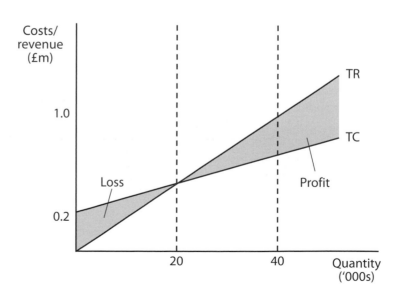

Stage 3

The point where the TR and TC lines cross is the breakeven level of output. At this point the firm will break even. Any level of output above this point means the firm will make a profit, but any level of output below this point means it will make a loss. This can be seen from the breakeven chart below.

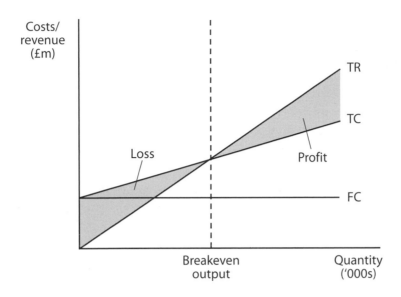

Stage 4

The firm's **margin of safety** can also be illustrated on the chart. This shows how far the firm's current output is from the breakeven. In other words, it shows how much output could fall before the firm started making a loss. The margin of safety is shown on the chart below.

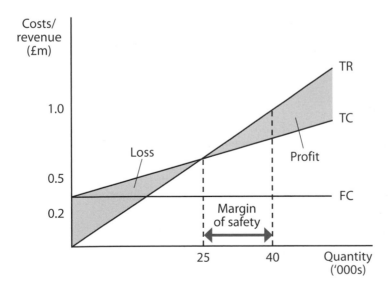

REVISION QUESTIONS

1. Define the term 'breakeven'.

2. What is meant by the term 'margin of safety'?

3. A factory has the capacity to produce 400,000 litres of shampoo per month. The shampoo sells for £2 per unit and the variable costs are £1.20 per unit. The company's fixed costs are £140,000 per month. Existing sales are 300,000 litres per month.
   (a) Calculate the breakeven in units and sales.
   (b) Calculate the level of sales required to make a profit of £120,000 per month.
   (c) If variable costs increase by 5%, what level of sales will be required to break even?
   (d) Calculate the margin of safety for the factory.

4. The Hard Stuff Company can produce 400,000 litres of a new non-alcoholic cocktail per month. The selling price is estimated at £4 per litre and the variable costs are estimated at £2.40 per unit. Fixed costs are £144,000 per month. Assume existing sales are £500,000 per month.
   (a) Calculate the breakeven in units and sales.
   (b) Calculate the level of sales required to make a profit of £270,000 per month.

5. A toy manufacturer can sell all the toys he produces each month, the selling price of each toy is £25, and the variable costs are £10 per unit. The fixed costs of running the business are £4,500 per month.
   (a) How many toys must be sold each month for the business to break even?
   (b) Current production is 400 toys per month. What is the profit?

6. A bakery can produce 500,000 loaves of bread per month. The loaves sell for £3 each, as they are organic. The variable costs are £1.50 per unit. The fixed costs are £450,000 per month.
   (a) Calculate the breakeven in units and sales.
   (b) Calculate the level of sales required to make a profit of £500,000 per month.
   (c) Calculate the margin of safety, and draw a traditional breakeven graph. Assume the existing sales are £1 million per month.

7. A pizza parlour currently produces 5,000 pizzas per week. The selling price of the pizzas is £2.45. The variable costs are £1.50 per unit. The fixed costs are £2,750 per week.
   (a) Calculate the breakeven in units and sales.
   (b) What is the margin of safety?
   (c) How many pizzas would the parlour have to bake per week to earn a profit of £10,000?
   (d) Draw a traditional breakeven graph.
   (e) If the variable costs were £1.75 per unit, how many pizzas would the company have to bake per week to break even?

8. The Hotel's Friend is a professional laundry company. It launders 20,000 sheets per week. The company charges £1.15 for every sheet laundered. Dervla, the manager, reckons that the variable costs are £0.57 per unit. The fixed costs are £7,400 per week.
   (a) Calculate the breakeven both by sales value and number of units.
   (b) How many sheets would the company have to launder per week to make a profit of £25,000?

(c) If Dervla increases the charge per sheet to £1.60, how many sheets would the company have to launder per week to break even? Calculate the breakeven from a traditional breakeven chart.

9. A winery manufactures wine racks that sell for £5.40 each. The variable costs are £3 per unit, and the fixed costs are £1,400 per month. The company currently sells 1,200 racks per month.
   (a) Calculate the company's breakeven in units.
   (b) Calculate the company's margin of safety.
   (c) How many racks would the company need to sell to make a profit of £7,000 per month?
   (d) Draw a traditional breakeven chart for the company.

10. Delta Ltd has produced the following statement for the month of December 2004.

Budgeted output	400,000 units
Selling price	£40 per unit
Variable costs	£28 per unit
Fixed costs	£960,000

   (a) Calculate the breakeven in units and in sales and illustrate this using a breakeven graph.
   (b) How many units must be produced to make a profit of £800,000?
   (c) The directors of the company are considering reducing the selling price by 10% per unit. Marketing estimates that this will increase the number of units being sold by 15%. Should the company proceed with this? (All workings must be shown).

11. What are the limitations of breakeven analysis?

12. A hotel has fixed costs of £32,000 per month. The average spending per guest is £36 per night, with a variable cost of £10 per guest per night. The hotel has accommodation for 60 guests. Assume the average month has 30 nights.
   (a) Prepare a breakeven chart showing the number of guests that have to stay in the hotel each month in order for it to break even.
   (b) How many guests have to stay in the hotel to achieve a profit of £3,000 per month?
   (c) How much profit or loss is made if 1,000 guests stay at the hotel during one particular month?

13. A pizzeria has fixed costs of £4,600 per month. This covers rent, rates, insurance, depreciation, and the fixed elements of labour and fuel charges. All other costs are regarded as variable. Variable costs are calculated as 15% of sales. The average spend per pizza is £2.80.
   (a) Use the contribution method to calculate how many pizzas must be sold each month for the establishment to break even.
   (b) Calculate how many pizzas must be sold each month for the establishment to make a profit of:
      (i) £1,200
      (ii) £1,900

CHAPTER 7

Budgets

A **budget** is a plan that is drawn up setting out revenues or costs (or both) for a given period of time. Most budgets are drawn up for the financial year and are usually broken down into shorter time periods such as months.

©iStockphoto.com/kutay tanir

The budget allows comparisons to be made between actual results and what was budgeted, to assess how an organisation has been performing. The differences between the two figures are known as **variances** and these can be either **adverse** or **favourable**. Budgets are therefore useful tools to help an organisation become more effective.

Although budgets are expressed in monetary terms, showing the income and expenditure needed during a financial period, they may be initially calculated using quantities such as labour hours or kilograms of materials.

Interrelationship of budgets

Budgets are drawn up for individual departments and functional areas, and are interrelated, as illustrated by this diagram.

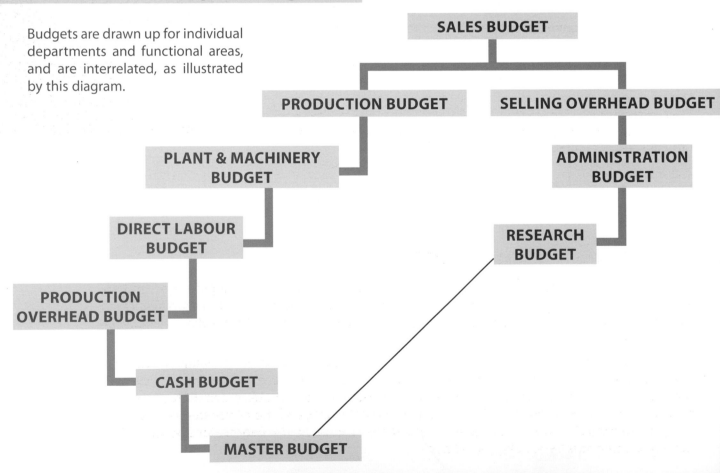

For example, Zeemobile Ltd produces mobile phones. The sales director has estimated that the following quantities will be sold in the next six months.

	Jan	Feb	Mar	Apr	May	Jun
Sales	2,000	2,400	3,000	3,200	3,200	3,500

The production department will manufacture these mobiles in the month before the sales take place, and it has been agreed to maintain a stock of 400 mobiles at any one time. On 1 December this stock was 200 mobiles.

The first step that management should take is to draw up a table providing all of this information.

	Dec	Jan	Feb	Mar	Apr	May	Jun
Opening stock	200	2,400	2,800	3,400	3,600	3,600	3,900
Production	2,200	2,400	3,000	3,200	3,200	3,500	
Sales		2,000	2,400	3,000	3,200	3,200	1,750
Closing stock	2,400	2,800	3,400	3,600	3,600	3,900	

©iStockphoto.com/phildate

This table clearly shows how many mobiles need to be produced each month. Once this information has been calculated, management needs to consider the decisions the production manager must take and which budgets these decisions will affect.

One of the first decisions that needs to be made is whether or not the organisation has the capacity to produce these mobiles. This will involve assessing the machine capacity of the organisation and looking at the current labour situation of the firm. The reason for assessing these factors is that more machines and labour may be required, especially in the busier months. If this is the case, the budgets associated with these areas will be affected and the accountant will need to look at any cash requirements to meet these changes.

These changes will be reflected in the **cash budget**. It is therefore clear that a change in one budget can have an effect on other budgets.

Approaches to budgeting

When drawing up budgets, there are different approaches that may be adopted. A *top-down* approach to budget setting would involve the owners or directors of an organisation deciding on the individual plans for each department. These plans are then given to the individual managers to implement.

Other organisations prefer to adopt a *bottom-up* approach. This is when individual managers draw up their own budgets and these are given to the owners or directors who coordinate the individual budgets into a **master budget**. In such a case a budget committee may be formed, made up of all the functional or departmental managers. The committee reviews the budgets submitted by individual managers and there may need to be negotiations between the functional areas to introduce budget changes.

Types of budgets

There are a number of different types of budgets. A **fixed budget** is not changed, even when the actual activity levels differ from those originally set. A **flexible budget** is one which is changed to allow for the behaviour of variable costs at different levels of activity.

Additionally, budgets can be classified as **incremental budgets** (also known as historic budgets) or **zero-based budgets**. Incremental budgeting simply involves taking the previous year's budget figures and adding on percentage increases, either for inflation or where circumstances demand it. Zero-based budgeting is often used in a new or unstable business. Each time a new budget is drawn up it is not based on the previous year, but is based on entirely new costings and projections.

©iStockphoto.com/Maica

Budget variances

Once a budget is set it will be monitored and the actual results will be compared with the budgeted results. As stated earlier, any differences are known as variances and management needs to examine the extent of these. If the variances are relatively small no action might be necessary. It is important that management not only identifies the variances but that it assesses the cause of the variance and takes remedial action.

Variances can be favourable, when the actual results are better that the budgeted results, or they can be adverse, when they are worse.

For example, a favourable sales variance will occur if sales are better than budgeted, and an adverse sales variance will occur if sales are worse than budgeted. A favourable labour variance will occur if labour costs are better than budgeted, and a negative labour variance will occur if labour costs are worse than budgeted.

ACTIVITY 7.1

Investigate the following cost figures for a manufacturing company.

	Budgeted cost £	Actual cost £
Materials	60,000	55,000
Labour	100,000	120,000
Overheads	25,000	24,000
Total cost	185,000	199,000

1. Calculate the variances for each cost.
2. Identify if they are adverse or favourable.
3. Suggest some factors which might have caused each of the variances.

Benefits of budgeting

There is a range of benefits to an organisation of drawing up a budget:

- Budgeting allows an organisation to control both its income and its expenditure, and can highlight areas where it is not performing as efficiently as it could. Budgeting is therefore a useful control mechanism for an organisation.
- Budgets are a useful way of clarifying the roles and responsibilities of management within an organisation.
- Budgets help to coordinate the activities of an organisation and can improve the communication between departments.
- Budgets help to ensure that scarce resources are used as efficiently as possible.
- Budgets enable performance to be measured against set targets.
- Budgets can help to motivate employees.

Disadvantages of budgeting

There are also some disadvantages associated with budgeting:

- Budgeting is dependant upon the quality of the information provided. Poor-quality information results in budgets that are meaningless.
- Budgets can become very inflexible.
- Budgets can be demotivating if the users have not been involved in the budgeting process.
- There can be a danger of management becoming overdependent on budgets at the expense of managing.

Cash budgets

All of the main budgets contribute to the firm's cash budget which in turn provides the data for the master budget (the forecasted financial statements). The cash budget is therefore central to all organisations.

Cash budgets (also known as **cash flow forecasts**) are drawn up to outline the expected cash or bank receipts and payments for a business, usually on a month-by-month basis. A balance is shown each month and this allows the business to forecast periods when outgoings are higher than incomings.

A cash budget may be defined as a forecast of receipts and payments which is normally prepared on a monthly basis for the budget period.

It is not sufficient to make a profit. Managers must also ensure that the business has adequate cash because one of the main causes of bankruptcy is poor cash management.

The two main elements of the cash budget are the forecasts and the timing of funds.

©iStockphoto.com/jsmith

ITEMS INCLUDED IN A CASH BUDGET

Receipts are any items of cash received. Payments are any items paid for in cash. The cash budget for a month, quarter, or year, will only include items that affect the company's cash or bank balance.

The following table shows some typical receipts and payments.

Receipts	Payments
Cash receipts	Payment for purchases
Debtor receipts	Overheads
Interest received	Tax
Tax refund	Drawings

Depreciation is *not* included in a cash budget. This is because no cash payment is ever made for depreciation.

☐ USES OF A CASH BUDGET

There are many reasons why cash budgets are drawn up:

- Management can forecast cash balances, and identify any cash shortages or surpluses.
- Cash budgets are forecasts, so management can easily ask "What if?" questions, for example "What if we had to pay creditors within three weeks?"
- If a cash budget reveals that a large bank overdraft is required, the company may consider revising its budgeted projections.

©iStockphoto.com/Aseev

☐ THE DIFFERENCE BETWEEN CASH AND PROFIT

The trading/profit and loss account focuses on the profit or gain after all expenses have been paid. The cash budget focuses on managing the cash flow in a business.

The closing cash balance for any month is not the same as the net profit for the month. It is a forecast of the cash or money available to pay suppliers and wages.

☐ THE TIMING OF RECEIPTS AND PAYMENTS

The cash budget is concerned with the timing of cash receipts and payments. For example, if the sales figures for January were £1,000 and the sales receipts for January were £1,500, why might this be the case? Similarly, if purchases for January were £900 and the payments for purchases were £600, why might this be the case?

©iStockphoto.com/diane39

ACTIVITY 7.2

Sales for January were £5,000 – 20% of this was **cash sales** and 80% was paid for one month later.

The timing of the receipts was as follows:

Jan   £1,000
Feb   £4,000

How would the following transactions be recorded?

1. Sales for February were £10,000, 15% of this was cash sales, and the remainder was received two months later.

2. Purchases for March were £5,000, 50% of this must be paid for in cash, and the remainder is paid for one month later.

3. Sales for January were £3,500, 10% of this was cash sales, 20% was received one month later, and the remainder was received two months later.

4. Purchases for February were £8,000, 5% of this was paid for up front, 10% was paid for one month later, and the balance was paid for two months later.

5. In January, Bob had sales of £15,000, 40% of this was paid in cash, and the balance was paid for one month later. (Bob is also due money from sales in December, sales in December were £10,000 and 50% of this sum is due to be received one month later.)

◻ PREPARING A CASH BUDGET

Steps 1 and 2 below are the planning or rough work stages. Attention to these should make Step 3 a lot easier to complete.

1. Prepare a sales schedule.
   (This is a plan of the monthly sales and then monthly receipts.)

2. Prepare a purchases schedule.
   (This is a plan of monthly purchases and then monthly payments for purchases.)

3. Prepare the actual cash budget.

A cash budget is normally set out as illustrated below.

©iStockphoto.com/peepo

Title			
	Jan	**Feb**	**Mar**
Receipts *eg debtors*			
Total receipts			
Payments *eg drawings*			
Total payments			
Receipts *less* payments			
Opening bank balance			
Closing bank balance			

The table below is an example of a cash budget.

Cash budget for BBA Ltd for June, July, August

	June £	July £	August £
Receipts:			
Cash sales	7,000	6,000	5,000
Debtors	54,000	45,000	63,000
Total receipts	61,000	51,000	68,000
Payments:			
Purchases	30,000	25,000	35,000
Wages	12,000	10,000	9,000
Overheads	12,000	16,000	14,000
Commission	2,250	3,150	2,700
Loan repayment	25,000		
Machine		15,000	15,000
Total payments	**81,250**	**69,150**	**75,700**
Receipts less payments	(20,250)	(18,150)	(7,700)
Opening bank balance	**22,000**	**1,750**	**(16,400)**
Closing bank balance	**1,750**	**(16,400)**	**(24,100)**

It is important to note that in this example the business had an opening bank balance of £22,000. It should also be noted that the closing bank balance of one month becomes the opening bank balance of the next month.

MANAGING CASH DEFICITS

It is not enough to identify cash deficits – managers must know how to manage situations where cash deficits may arise. There are many ways of doing this, including the following:

- Leasing instead of buying equipment
- Delaying the purchase of equipment
- Shortening the average debtor collection period
- Reducing stock levels
- Asking suppliers to extend credit periods

However, all of the above have both advantages and disadvantages.

ACTIVITY 7.3

Evaluate the advantages and disadvantages of the above solutions to managing cash deficits.

ACTIVITY 7.4

1. (a) You are the manager of a local health club, and have been asked to prepare the cash budget for the next quarter, ending in September 2004. The details are as follows:

- The projected cash balance at 1 July is £10,000.
- The actual sales for May and June were £6,000 and £9,000 respectively. The forecasted sales for July, August and September are £6,000, £7,000 and £5,000 respectively. Cash sales accounted for 90% of revenues, with 10% being received two months after the month of sale.
- Additional sales revenues of cosmetic health goods are forecasted at £600, £800 and £1,200 in the months of July, August and September (all for cash).
- Payments are forecasted at £6,000 for July and at £6,000 for August, and the forecast allocations are as follows:

     Overheads 40%

     Payments to creditors 60%

     All payments are made in the month they are incurred..
- A VAT repayment is forecasted to be received in July, amounting to £200.
- The club borrowed money to pay for equipment during the year – the first repayment of this loan will be paid in September, amounting to £100.
- A purchase of equipment is planned for September, costing £450, to be paid for in cash.
- Bank charges amounting to £25 were paid in September.

   (b) Discuss the options available to the health club manager in the event of any cash shortages.

2. (a) Read the following information carefully. You are required to prepare a cash budget for Trotters Independent Traders for the months of March, April, May and June only.

Month	Wages £	Materials £	Overheads £	Sales £
February	12,000	40,000	20,000	60,000
March	16,000	60,000	24,000	80,000
April	20,000	50,000	32,000	120,000
May	18,000	70,000	28,000	100,000
June	24,000	60,000	36,000	140,000

- Depreciation is estimated at £750 a month.
- Wages are paid for within the month they are incurred (the same month).
- Materials are paid for two months after delivery.
- 25% of monthly sales are for cash, 75% of sales are paid for two months later.
- Overheads are paid for one month later.
- The opening cash balance will be £11,000.

   (b) What would you advise the management of Trotters Independent Traders to do if the company is short of cash for any month?

Ratio formulae

☐ PROFITABILITY RATIOS

Gross profit margin

(gross profit/sales) × 100%

Net profit margin

(net profit/sales) × 100% = (profit before interest and taxation/sales) × 100%

Return on capital employed (ROCE)

(net profit/capital employed) × 100%

(capital employed = long–term loan + share capital + reserves)

Fixed asset turnover

sales/fixed assets

☐ INVESTMENT RATIOS

Gearing %

(long-term debt/capital employed) x 100%

Earnings per share (EPS)

profit available to ordinary shareholders /number of ordinary shares

Dividend per share (DPS)

dividends/number of ordinary shares

LIQUIDITY (EFFICIENCY) RATIOS

Current ratio

current assets/current liabilities = x:1

Acid test (quick ratio)

(current assets – closing stock)/current liabilities = x:1

Stock turnover

(average stock x 365 days)/cost of goods sold = stock turnover (days)

(cost of goods sold = (opening stock + purchases) – closing stock/2)

or

cost of goods sold/average stock

Average debtor collection period

(debtors x 365 days)/credit sales = debtors' collection period (days)

Average creditor repayment period

(creditors x 365 days)/credit purchases =creditors' repayment period (days)

Breakeven analysis formulae

Breakeven in units

fixed costs/contribution per unit

Breakeven in sales

(fixed costs/contribution per unit) $\times$ sales price per unit

To earn a target profit in units

(fixed cost + target profit)/contribution per unit

To earn a target profit in sales (£,000)

(fixed cost + target profit)/contribution per unit $\times$ sales price per unit

Profit volume ratio

contribution per unit/sales price per unit

Margin of safety

The percentage of existing or expected sales that may decrease before the company incurs a loss.

existing or expected sales – breakeven sales/existing or expected sales $\times$ 100%

Accounting terms

Absorption costing – charging or 'absorbing' all of the relative direct and indirect costs associated with business operations to a particular cost centre

Accrual (amount owing) – expenses that are outstanding at the end of an accounting period

Acid test ratio – a liquidity ratio that examines the relationship between current assets (less stock) and current liabilities

Adverse variance – the difference between planned and actual performance which causes the profit to be lower than budgeted

Assets – resources that are owned by a business

Bad debt – an amount owed to a business that is considered to be unrecoverable

Balance sheet – a statement of the financial position of an organisation that shows the assets of a business against the liabilities of the business

Breakeven – the point at which a firm neither makes a profit nor a loss

Budget – a plan that is drawn up setting out revenues or costs (or both) for a given period of time

Business angels – informal investors who are looking to invest in new and growing businesses in return for a share of the equity

Capital – money contributed to the business by the owner

Cash budget – a forecast of receipts and payments which is normally prepared on a monthly basis for the budget period

Cash flow forecast – another name for a cash budget

Cash purchases – purchases of goods that are paid for immediately

Cash sales – sales that are paid for immediately by cash or by cheque

Contribution – selling price per unit – variable cost per unit

Cost centre – an area, object, person or activity for which costs are separately collected

Cost of goods sold – opening stock + purchases – closing stock

Credit purchases – purchases of goods that may be paid for within an agreed time period

Credit sales – sales that are paid for by customers within a stated period of time

Creditors – suppliers to whom the business owes money

Current assets – items owned by a business that are retained for the short term, for example stock, debtors and cash

Current liabilities – amounts owed by a business that are to be repaid within 12 months

Debentures – loans that are usually secured. A secured debenture is one that is specifically tied to the financing of a particular asset such as a building or a machine.

Debtors – customers who owe the firm money

Depreciation – the estimate of the amount of the fall in the value of fixed assets over a stated period of time

Direct costs – costs that can be identified with a specific product or project, for example raw materials, packaging and direct labour

Discount factor – the rate applied to future cash flows to derive the present value of the cash flows

Discount allowed – the amount of cash given by a business to encourage debtors to pay promptly

Discount received – the amount of cash discount taken by a business when it settles its creditors promptly

Dividends – the proportion of profit paid to shareholders

Drawings – amounts (money or goods) taken out of a business by the owner for their own use

Earnings per share (EPS) – an investment ratio that shows the amount each share is earning for the shareholder

Equity – ordinary shares and reserves of a company

Factoring – a service offered by a financial institution which involves it taking over the trade debtors of a business

Favourable variance – the difference between planned and actual performance which causes the profit to be higher than budgeted

Fixed assets – items owned by a business that are retained for the long term, for example premises, equipment and motor vehicles

Fixed budget – a budget that is not changed, even when the actual activity levels differ from those set

Fixed costs – costs that remain the same irrespective of output levels

Flexible budget – a budget which is changed to allow for the behaviour of variable costs at different levels of activity

Gearing ratio – a ratio that relates the contribution of long-term lenders to the total long-term capital of a business

Gross profit – sales – cost of goods sold

Gross profit margin ratio – a profitability ratio that shows the relationship between the gross profit and the sales of an organisation

Hire-purchase (HP) – allows a business to use an asset such as a computer or a photocopier without having to pay for it all initially

Incremental budgeting – involves taking the previous year's budget figures and adding on percentage increases, either for inflation, or where circumstances demand it

Indirect costs – costs which are associated with the whole business. They can be referred to as overheads and can include rent, insurance, salaries of office staff, and rates

Leverage - the US term for Gearing

Liabilities – amounts that are owed by a business

Limited Company - A legal form of business (incorporated), which is owned by shareholders each of whom has part ownership of the business (shares) and whose liability for the debts of the business is limited to the value of those shares

Long-term liabilities – amounts that are owed by a business but are not liable for repayment within 12 months

Margin of safety – how far above breakeven output the firm is currently producing

Master budgets – a summary of the individual budgets drawn up

Mortgage – a loan secured on property

Net present value (NPV) – a method of investment appraisal based on the present value of all relevant cash flows associated with a project

Net profit – gross profit – expenses

Net profit margin ratio – a profitability ratio that shows the relationship between the net profit and the sales of an organisation

Ordinary shares – shares of a company owned by those who are due benefits of the company's activities after all other stakeholders have been paid

Partnership - An unincorporated business owned by two or more people

Payback period – the time taken for the initial investment in a project to be repaid

Preference shares – shares in a company that are owned by those who are entitled to the first part of any dividend that a company may pay

Prepayment – the part of an expense which is paid in advance for the next month or the next year

Profit – the amount of money 'made' as a result of business activities

Profit and loss account – a financial statement that shows the amount of profit or loss made by an organisation

Provision (allowance) for bad debts – the estimate by a business of the likely percentage of its debtors which may go bad during any one accounting period

Purchase returns (or returns outwards) – when a business returns goods to one of its suppliers

Reducing balance method – a method of calculating depreciation that uses a fixed percentage rate of depreciation each year

Return on capital employed (ROCE) – a profitability ratio that shows the profitability of a business in relation to the amount of capital employed

Sales returns (or returns inwards) – goods that have been sold by a firm and then have been returned by customers

Semi-variable costs – costs that have an element of both fixed and variable costs

Share – a portion of the ownership of a company

Sole trader – an individual trading in his or her name, or under a suitable trading name

Specific bad debt (bad debts written off) – debts that a business is not able to collect and is certain that the debtor will not or cannot pay

Straight-line method – a method of accounting for depreciation that allocates the amount to be depreciated evenly over the life span of the asset

Stocks - a firm's stocks of raw materials, work in progress, and finished goods. An alternative word is 'Inventory'

Total costs – fixed costs +variable costs

Trading/profit and loss account – a financial statement that shows the amount of profit or loss made by a merchandising organisation

Variable costs – costs that change as output levels change

Variance – the difference between planned and actual performance. *See also adverse variance and favourable variance*

Working capital – current assets – current liabilities

Zero-based budgeting – often used in a new or unstable business. Each time a new budget is drawn up it is not based on the previous year, but is based on entirely new costings and projections.